a**thankful**heart

carole lewis

Regal

From Gospel Light
Ventura, California, U.S.A.

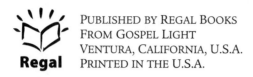

PUBLISHED BY REGAL BOOKS
FROM GOSPEL LIGHT
VENTURA, CALIFORNIA, U.S.A.
PRINTED IN THE U.S.A.

Regal Books is a ministry of Gospel Light, a Christian publisher dedicated to serving the local church. We believe God's vision for Gospel Light is to provide church leaders with biblical, user-friendly materials that will help them evangelize, disciple and minister to children, youth and families.

It is our prayer that this Regal book will help you discover biblical truth for your own life and help you meet the needs of others. May God richly bless you.

For a free catalog of resources from Regal Books/Gospel Light, please call your Christian supplier or contact us at 1-800-4-GOSPEL *or* www.regalbooks.com.

Library of Congress Cataloging-in-Publication Data
Lewis, Carole, 1942-
  A thankful heart / Carole Lewis.
    p. cm.
  ISBN 0-8307-3804-5 (hard cover)
  1. Christian women—Religious life.   2. Gratitude—Religious aspects—
Christianity. I. Title.
BV4527.L49 2005
248.8'43—dc22   2005019949

1   2   3   4   5   6   7   8   9   10   /   10   09   08   07   06   05

Rights for publishing this book in other languages are contracted by Gospel Light Worldwide, the international nonprofit ministry of Gospel Light. Gospel Light Worldwide also provides publishing and technical assistance to international publishers dedicated to producing Sunday School and Vacation Bible School curricula and books in the languages of the world. For additional information, visit www.gospellightworldwide.org; write to Gospel Light Worldwide, P.O. Box 3875, Ventura, CA 93006; or send an e-mail to info@gospellightworldwide.org.

Contents

Introduction

Dear Friends:

I want to show you a Scripture verse that contains the key to living an extraordinary life:

> Give thanks in all circumstances, for this is God's will for you in Christ Jesus (1 Thess. 5:18).

Have you ever thought about how radical this verse is?

Living a life characterized by thankfulness is not natural to our human condition. It is much easier to stuff our lives with complaints, anger, frustration and despair. But what benefit do those attitudes bring? A life that wallows in darkness is only harmful to the person living it and to the ones he or she loves.

What is required to live a thankful life is a paradigm shift—a transformation of the way we view the world around us and the circumstances of our lives. If we are to develop a lifestyle that brings hope and healing, we must consciously look for the positive and reject the temptation to dwell on the negative.

This isn't always easy to do. When we begin to live a lifestyle of thankfulness, it soon becomes obvious that it is not a task we can accomplish in our own strength and power. We also soon learn that thankfulness is both a one-time commitment and a decision we make every day. Choosing to give thanks becomes what defines our moments. At each juncture of our lives, we can either decide to trust that God is working all things together for our good or we can fall back into self-pity and begin questioning God's faithfulness.

The results of living a life of thankfulness are well worth it. Will you join me on this journey?

I hope you will!

Carole Lewis

A Breath of Fresh Thankfulness

*Give thanks in all circumstances, for this is
God's will for you in Christ Jesus.*

1 THESSALONIANS 5:18

Have you ever noticed how incredibly easy it is to focus on what's wrong with life?

Good moments are easy to treasure. Weddings, the birth of a baby, children doing well in school, enough money to pay the bills—few of us would question that these are all occasions to give God thanks.

It is quite another thing to give thanks when life isn't going so well. I'm not necessarily talking about the big, bad events. I'm talking about how easy it is for even the ordinary irritations of life to build into occasions for continual grumbling and dissatisfaction. Let me show you what I mean. Have you ever had a day like this?

> *It can't be 6:30 A.M. already. Groan. Another day . . .
> here we go.*
> *Good grief! The kitchen floor is sticky. I feel like a cleaning
> machine around here.*
> *Oh no! I could have sworn these pants still fit. Why even
> try to eat healthy?*
> *"Hey watch it, buddy!" This traffic sure is driving me
> crazy today.*

Ooh! There's Alice, coming straight to my desk. She never has anything good to say about anybody.

Not the phone again! How can I get anything done with all these distractions?

No groceries in the house, nothing to cook—I guess we'll have to eat out again.

"Kids! How many times do I have to tell you to turn off the TV and do your homework?!"

Sometimes it seems like there are more bad moments than good in life. The problem is that if we don't stop and take a clear look at our perceptions of these situations, pretty soon we find that we have bitter, negative experiences all day long. Soon enough, having negative experiences all day long turns into having negative experiences every day, every year, every decade. One morning we wake up and discover that these experiences have transformed us. It isn't the situations that are negative now—it's us. We've become bitter, negative people.

And we hate who we've become.

I've found it to be a simple truth—when I do not practice developing a thankful heart, the person this hurts the most is me. I want you to try an experiment: Walk around with a furrowed brow all day and see what happens. Chances are, you'll end up with a headache by the time you go to bed and you'll also feel the stress of having had absolutely no pleasant interactions with other people that day. Notch this up another level.

Gripe about your job for a week and see how long you stay employed. Or snap at your husband every night when he comes home and see what sort of marriage it produces. It's in our best interest to not fall into the trap of focusing on what's wrong with life. Becoming a thankful person is a benefit to our lives that we absolutely cannot overlook.

The effects of focusing on the negative can hurt us more than we may realize. Have you ever heard that a link exists between emotional health and our physical health? It's true, God created our minds and our bodies to communicate with each other. When we're embarrassed (something that happens in our mind), our faces go red (something that happens to our body). When we're nervous (mind), we get sweaty hands or butterflies in our stomachs (body). When we're angry, our blood pressure rises. These are examples of how what we think and feel can affect us. If we choose to have negative attitudes for much of our day, that spills over and damages our health and well-being. Grumbling only hurts us.

11

God knows how dangerous complaining can be. When He brought Israel out of slavery from Egypt, Scripture tells us that one of the Israelites' most noticeable sins was ungratefulness. Instead of voicing praise to God for delivering them from their cruel taskmasters, the Israelites complained continually about everything that happened to them. Food, shelter, water, direction—if it wasn't one thing it was another.

Finally, God had had enough. Numbers 14:26-29 records these shocking words:

> The Lord said to Moses and Aaron: "How long will this wicked community grumble against me? I have heard the complaints of these grumbling Israelites. So tell them, 'As surely as I live, declares the Lord, I will do to you the very things I heard you say: In this desert your bodies will fall—every one of you.'"

God takes grumbling seriously—and it's not just the Israelites to whom God gives strong warnings about ungratefulness. Philippians 2:14 tells us, "Do everything without complaining." James 5:9 says, "Don't grumble against each other." Proverbs 19:3 says, "A man's own folly ruins his life." Giving thanks is serious business. Thanksgiving is the language and vocabulary of the Bible. It's a language and vocabulary that we may be unfamiliar with, but it's something we desperately need to learn.

Hope Comes on the Side of a Road

Almost 10 years ago, a young woman named Branda Polk taught me a wonderful truth I have never forgotten.

We were set to teach at a First Place Conference in North Carolina in the middle of winter. (First Place is a

Christ-centered health program that emphasizes balance in the physical, mental, emotional and spiritual areas of life.) I remember that it was absolutely freezing that year. The workshop was ready to begin, but Branda was nowhere in sight. It wasn't like Branda to not be on time. I began to glance at my watch every few minutes and prayed silently that she hadn't come to any harm. The first session finished and Branda still had not arrived.

Suddenly Branda burst through the door. She gave me a grin that said everything was just fine. "You'll never believe what just happened to me," she exclaimed.

Everything was on schedule when Branda's plane had landed. She retrieved her bags and secured her rental car to drive to the workshop. After driving a few miles out of the city, she heard a clunk, clunk, clunk against the snowy freeway that could only mean one thing. The rental car had a flat tire.

13

Right there on the side of the road, Branda began to pray. She had decided to follow God's word found in 1 Thessalonians 5:18—to give thanks in all circumstances. So she thanked God that she had on a warm jacket and boots. She thanked God that she was able to pull way off the busy freeway as soon as she heard the clunk and would be in no danger of getting hit from behind by another car. She thanked God that her dad had taught her how to change a flat tire and that she was physically fit enough to accomplish the task.

She finished praying, opened the trunk and began to dig for the jack.

Just then, a pickup truck pulled over and a friendly looking farmer got out to offer help. While the man changed the tire, Branda discovered that he was a believer in Jesus Christ.

"I was driving along and something just told me you could use a hand," he said to Branda.

It's not always that God sends us answers to prayer that we don't even pray. But what impressed me so much about Branda's situation was that she chose to give thanks for whatever she could, right in the middle of a difficult situation—even if that meant changing the tire herself.

Friends, that's the secret of living life well. We can bring an attitude of thankfulness to any experience; and when we do, it's like a breath of fresh air rushing in and blowing away the dust of decay. Some people possess an attitude of gratitude more naturally than others. But all of us are called to step onto this path. That's what this book discusses at length. As we learn to cultivate a thankful heart, our grumbling and complaining will cease and be replaced by a spirit that blesses God, blesses those around us and even blesses ourselves. There is an answer to the question of what to do when life doesn't go perfectly: Give thanks in every situation in life.

That may be a concept you've never heard before. Giving thanks throughout each moment, each day, each week, and each year is something few of us have been encouraged to do. Maybe you're saying right now that it can't be done. You've lived through experiences too horrific to be able to give thanks. Life has thrown you some unfair curveballs and there are huge black clouds hovering over seasons in your past. Perhaps right now as you read this book you're experiencing enormous pain in your life. It's hard for you to get up and get dressed each morning, much less try to give thanks for anything.

My friend, if that is your situation, there is hope. I also know a sorrow too inexpressible for words. I know firsthand how it's one thing to be able to give thanks amidst the small inconveniences of life, but when your world caves in around you, giving thanks is another thing entirely.

If you've read any of my other books, you've probably heard this story before. But I tell it again because this experience is so deeply ingrained in who I am today. Of all ironies, my family's greatest tragedy happened on Thanksgiving Day. This darkness happened four years ago from this writing, but it's as clear as if it happened yesterday.

Let me explain.

A Day of Thanksgiving, a Day of Pain

The remains of the turkey had long since been put in the fridge. The last of the mashed potatoes had been scooped up. One or two pieces of pumpkin pie listed in pans on the counter. Thanksgiving Day 2001 was almost over.

I had decided to go to bed early. Stopping in the living room, I took one last look at the Christmas tree my daughter Shari had decorated hours earlier. It was a 10-year tradition with us. My husband, Johnny, and I live on Galveston Bay, so our family always decorates with a nautical theme. Every year, right after Thanksgiving dinner, Shari and I would bring down fishnet, swags, buoys and sailboats from the attic and begin to plan for the festivities surrounding Christ's birth.

That day, after the tree was finished, Shari, her husband, Jeff, and their three girls, Cara, 19, Christen, 15, and Amanda, 13, left our home to celebrate Thanksgiving with Jeff's parents. It was quiet now except for Johnny and two of his brothers sitting outside on the patio talking. I went to bed and fell into an easy sleep. About 9:15 P.M. the phone rang. Instinctively, I reached for it in the dark and said hello.

16

Have you ever had one of those moments when life stands still? Something irreversibly changes and you don't quite yet fathom all that has happened, but you just know that an event has occurred after which nothing will be the same again.

It was Cara, my granddaughter, on the phone. She was screaming, crying uncontrollably. I could just make out "Mom" and "accident," but the rest was just a blur of words and emotion.

My son-in-law's brother, Ronnie, took the phone from Cara and pieced together the story

After dinner with Jeff's family, Shari, Jeff and the girls climbed in their Ford Expedition, preparing to drive back to their house for the night. Almost on second thought, Shari remembered something she wanted to leave with Jeff's mom. As she stood behind their SUV, another car careened down the street, swerved, hit a light pole and ricocheted into Shari, throwing her into the yard. The rest of the family, except for Christen, were still in the SUV and protected from the impact of the drunk driver. Shari was now on her way to the intensive care unit at the hospital.

Shari was our middle child. We have an older girl, Lisa, and our youngest is John. When Shari was a child, I used to read to her for hours on end. She loved books and she also loved playing mommy. She used to pray that the Lord wouldn't return before she could grow up and be a mommy herself. When she grew up and had her girls, she exhibited an incredible love and closeness for her children.

17

Our family was gathered in a hospital waiting room when the chaplain came in to tell us Shari was gone.

She was 39—wife to Jeff, mother to 3 girls. And she would always be my daughter. I knew she was in the Lord's presence, but I still felt an unspeakable pain. I wanted Shari back more than I could stand.

How could I ever be thankful in the midst of this?

In the days and months that followed, God did an incredible work in our family and in my life and heart. Life has a way of leveling our playing fields through the losses we experience, both great and small. I am convinced today that we cannot become the people God wants us to become unless we learn to accept what we cannot change. I know that I'm the woman I am today because of this horrific experience.

But to give thanks?

Yes.

Even for my afflictions?

Absolutely.

Can I actually say that Shari's death was part of God's perfect and good plan for our lives?

Without a doubt.

Living Beyond the Ashes

I promise you that if an attitude of gratitude is not already part of who you are, God can change your heart. When we begin to thank God in the middle of our situations—no matter what we're going through— our situations no longer appear hopeless, and we'll begin to see change.

In the pages ahead, we'll take a closer look at what it means to be thankful in all things. We may not always understand how thankfulness in the midst of a situation can make a difference, but it's up to us to step onto the path of gratefulness and begin to walk in its direction.

It is my prayer that as you read this book, God will teach you about Himself and why a thankful heart will not only change you but will also change your circumstances. Each of us has the opportunity to choose thankfulness in every situation in life, no matter how small or large the situation.

When we embrace this path—the path of God's truth—the fresh breath of gratefulness begins to filter through our lives by the power of His Holy Spirit. Gratefulness is God's will for us. The benefit for us is hope and healing.

If that's what you want in your life, I invite you to keep reading.

Prayer

Dear Lord, I don't understand how thankfulness in the midst of my situation can make a difference, but today I want to choose to be thankful. Show me things to be thankful for and remind me to thank You again and again until it becomes a part of who I am. Amen.

19

CHAPTER 2

Moments of Purpose

*For those God foreknew he also predestined to be con-
formed to the likeness of his Son.*

ROMANS 8:29

Years ago, I heard a powerful message by Gloria
Gaither. "Life is made up of moments," she said.
"Some are good, some are bad, and most of the time we
don't even know the difference."

I can relate. As recently as this morning, I was faced
with a choice of how I would view my commute to
work. Sounds simple, a nonissue really, but it illustrates exactly what Gloria is talking about.

This morning, rain fell with a vengeance. It was no
ordinary shower, this downpour. Water pummeled our
roof and rushed through the downspouts. It dropped
from the sky with such force that it bounced off our
driveway and seemed to come up as much as it came
down. I could feel concern rising in my chest. Driving
in heavy rain always makes me nervous.

A rainy workday—one moment in my life. Would it
be a good moment or a bad moment?

As I backed out of our driveway, I began to thank
God for the rain, because someone—somewhere—needed rain today. I asked His protection for everyone who
would be driving in the rain, including myself. (Have
you ever prayed for everyone in your city on their

morning commutes? God is big enough to handle such a prayer!) I thanked Him that I was able to drive in early, before the really heavy traffic occurred, and I thanked Him for creating a world so amazing that things like rain occur in the first place.

Before I knew it, I had arrived at the office and was closing my umbrella at the door. I felt refreshed and secure knowing that God was in control and that He cared for me. It was going to be a good day.

Today's rainy morning was a moment in time that will never repeat itself. It would have been so easy to allow the rain to spoil my day—or at least get it off to a bad start. But the power of thankfulness turned what could have been a negative moment into a positive one. Our perspective about what we go through, moment by moment, is paramount to the person we ultimately become.

A Life of Moments

Our lives comprise millions of moments—some good, some bad and some in between. Sometimes it feels as though we have more than our fair share of bad moments. Have you ever wished that all your moments could be good? It sure would be a lot simpler to give thanks in all things, wouldn't it!

When bad things happen to us, it is our natural tendency to lash out. I'm talking about when we rail at circumstances and tense up inside. We get taut in our spirit and begin to point at faults. We grumble about our nega-tive situation and say negative things about others who brought on the situation; or maybe we blame ourselves for being stupid or not foreseeing some consequence. Sometimes we even blame God, who is ultimately seen as the One responsible for our predicament.

Here's a moment I remember from when my chil-dren were little. One morning, Shari woke up with chewing gum stuck in her hair. Has that ever happened to one of your children? What a mess! You can pull and drag but it'll never come out. Your daughter will howl and protest, but she can't go to school with a big wad of Juicy Fruit stuck to her head. Cutting the hair is always an option, but the child will look like a patchy poodle. *May just serve her right,* you mutter under your breath. She shouldn't have disobeyed in the first place and gone to sleep while chewing gum.

22

How easy is it for us to gripe and complain when bad things happen, even something so small as chew-ing gum stuck to hair. Our day gets off to a bad start, we think, and so it's even easier to let other annoyances throughout the rest of the day gather and compound. By dinnertime, we're wound tighter than a drum. And look out, world! Anyone who gets in our way will get what he or she deserves.

By the way, peanut butter works pretty well. A friend mentioned it to me one day as the perfect gum-removal remedy. The next time my daughter Shari woke up with a wad of gum in her hair—and believe me, it happened more than once—I slathered the stuff on. *Voila!* No more gum. Who knew?

It's funny, but when I look back now, I am so thankful that I chose other paths when those gum-stuck moments happened with my daughter, even before I knew about the peanut butter remedy. Sure, there was a tendency to grumble, to become upset. But with Shari in heaven today, how thankful I am that I didn't scream or berate her every time she acted thoughtlessly. Those were learning moments for both my daughter and for me, as prized now as when she learned to ride her bike. The perspective of hindsight allows me to see those times with my daughter for what they truly were—absolutely precious.

23

God's Plan for Our Moments

There's a verse that helps me put all my moments—both good and bad—into perspective. Romans 8:29 says, "For those God foreknew he also predestined to be conformed to the likeness of His Son."

God has an amazing plan for us, and He uses the moments of our lives to fulfill His plan. God wants us to become like His Son, Jesus Christ. He wants to transform us—to change us—into people who live and act as Christ lives. God isn't content to leave us wallowing in our sins—He loves us too much for that. He wants to give us more than we could dare to ask or imagine. He wants to make us like Christ.

Developing a thankful heart is part of God's purpose for our moments. God wants us to look more and more like Christ every day we live. God wants us to think like Jesus, talk like Jesus and, yes, to act like Jesus. God wants us all to cultivate thankful hearts. God wants us to begin thanking Him in every situation in which we find ourselves.

How does God's transformation work? Two additional verses are helpful here. Romans 5:3-4 gives us the sequence: Our tribulations bring about perseverance, perseverance brings proven character, and character brings hope.

James 1:3-4 expands on this: Our testing produces perseverance (endurance); "Perseverance must finish its work so that you may be mature and complete, not lacking anything."

You see, friends, God is interested in the growth of our faith. One of the ways He does this is to allow a variety of experiences to come our way—both good and bad. In fact, one of the tools God uses to bring about transformation is tribulation. These trials are not given to us haphazardly. They're allowed to come into our lives by a great and loving God. There is a perfect purpose to them.

In fact, the original word for tribulation that Paul uses in Romans has the underlying meaning of being under pressure to yield something good. It was used to describe the process of squeezing olives in a press to produce olive oil, or grapes getting compressed to extract the juice. Our tribulations have a purpose, Scripture says. God has an end product in mind for us, and God's end product is like the finest oil or a nourishing drink. That's what God wants for our lives.

One of our longtime friends, Les O'Neal, is a great example of someone whom God has transformed over the years into the image of Christ.

When Les retired a couple of years ago, he immediately volunteered to work in the pastoral care department of our church. He spends most days now in the hospitals of Houston, Texas, visiting those who are hurting. He spends his days talking, praying and sometimes just sitting with people who are going through tough times. It's not always pleasant work. Being in a hospital around so many sick and hurting people can be taxing. Les has seen his share of wounds and blood; he has smelled disease and decay; he has cried with families in anguish.

25

Why would Les spend his time doing this? Why doesn't he play golf, Bingo or lay in the sun in Miami? Les's volunteer work is tangible proof that he has learned the art of cultivating a thankful heart. God has worked on Les over the years. God has molded him into someone who knows what true beauty is. It isn't that there's anything wrong with traveling or having hobbies in retirement years, but Les has chosen to spend his time being a blessing to others.

Without a doubt when Les arrives in heaven someday, God will look across expanses of glory and say to him, "Well done, my good and faithful servant."

Learning to cultivate thankfulness plays itself out in our daily lives as we speak blessings on others and as our lives become blessings to others for God's glory. God's will is for us to be His hands, His feet and His words to a lost and dying world. How desperately we need to be reminded that when we grumble or complain, it is God's will for us to speak blessings and to be a blessing to everyone we know.

Part of God's Plan

When it comes to the transforming work God does in our lives, He allows us the wonderful privilege of being a part of this work. God never drags us kicking and screaming to somewhere we don't want to go. He gives us free will—the ability to say yes and no, the capacity to obey or disobey.

Developing a thankful heart for all the moments in our lives, both good and bad, means that instead of ranting against the things we can't change, we choose to thank God. I believe that being thankful to God has the potential not only to alter our perception of our circumstances but also to heal our hearts during the most painful circumstances of life.

Ultimately, it is my prayer that every believer would glean hope and help from God while learning how to be thankful for every moment of life. But before we can begin to look at the bigger issues of our lives, we need to start thanking God for the everyday moments we all experience.

One of the most important moments of the day is when we turn off the alarm clock, signaling that a new day is beginning. What a perfect moment to start thanking God. Try this: Tomorrow morning when you wake up, thank God for everything you can think of. Your thanks may be something as straightforward as:

- Thanks, God, that I'm still alive.
- Thanks, God, that I can sit, stand and walk.
- Thanks, God, that I have a bed to sleep in with sheets and a blanket.
- Thanks, God, that I can enjoy a warm shower.

27

This exercise is a simple but powerful tool. When we start our day thanking God, we have set the tone for the entire day. We will never have another morning exactly like today, and this day is made up of moments that will never occur again. The sunrise will never look exactly like it looks today. The sun on our front lawn will never show the exact same colors. Learning to be thankful in small things will enable us to be thankful when the big challenges of life come to us.

This morning, like every morning, thankfulness is a choice. Practice thinking of daily irritations, such as spilled milk, forgotten lunches or homework assignments, as moments that in years to come will hold precious memories. You're on your way to cultivating a thankful heart. When you start small, like beginning each morning by thanking God, the small areas will gradually become larger and larger.

We can cultivate a thankful heart by speaking blessings on those with whom we come in contact each day. When someone cuts in front of us in traffic, we can ask God to bless him or her instead of railing against the person's lack of courtesy. We never know what other people are going through. By asking God to bless them, we are extending the same grace to them that God has extended to us.

Another way to cultivate a thankful heart is by consciously being a blessing to others. When we see people going through tough times, we can step in and lighten their load. It might be something as simple as helping retrieve a dropped bag of groceries scattered on a parking lot pavement or putting our arm around someone who has just received bad news.

One of the attributes that impresses me most about Bill Greig III, president of Gospel Light and publisher of my books, is his habit of verbally blessing me each time we meet together. Blessing people is actually thanking God for them. It's an act of gratefulness. Bill always has a word of encouragement for me. Whenever I receive an e-mail from Bill, it's signed "Blessings, Bill." Bill has learned to cultivate thankfulness, and it plays itself out in his daily life.

Bill told me a story about being taught thankfulness as a child. It was one of those small moments that laid the foundation for a lifestyle of thankfulness. When Bill was about to enter the sixth grade, he received news that his new teacher was the one that every child feared getting for his own. When Bill's dad came into his bedroom to say goodnight, he found Bill quite upset. When asked why, Bill announced that he was going to have the meanest teacher in his school that year.

Bill's dad sat on the side of his bed and said one sentence that has stayed with Bill to this day: "Bill, let's thank God right now for your teacher."

Bill couldn't believe his ears, but that night father and son prayed for Bill's new teacher and thanked God for her. Bill told me this teacher turned out to be the best he ever had during all his school years.

29

God doesn't always provide such a drastic change to our circumstances as that, but I believe the foundation for change can lie in the smallest of moments. As we seek to cultivate thankful hearts, the blessings of God open up to us. Whenever you and I feel the temptation to grumble and complain, we need to let the Lord remind us that His will for us is to speak blessings and to be a blessing to everyone we know.

Your Future Starts Now

Today, if an attitude of gratitude is not part of who you are, why not ask God to help you change. I believe that as you begin thanking God in the middle of your moments—good or bad—each situation will take on new color. Your bad situations will no longer appear hopeless, and your heart will also change. One of the ways this change comes about is to thank God for whatever you can in your present circumstance.

It may be difficult. In fact, at the beginning, your thoughts may be so negative that the subject matter of your prayers may only involve giving thanks for clean towels. That's perfectly fine. Start wherever you are. As you begin to cultivate gratefulness as a way of life, God will show you other things to be thankful for.

You can do it! Your future of gratefulness can begin right now.

Prayer

Dear Lord, I realize that moments are precious to You. Help me learn that moments can be precious to me too. Thank You for the moments of my life, both good and bad, and help me to be thankful for every moment, because they are Your gift to me. Amen.

A Shocking Preposition

*Always giving thanks to God the Father for everything,
in the name of our Lord Jesus Christ.*
EPHESIANS 5:20

Corrie ten Boom, in *The Hiding Place,* her famous book about life in a Nazi concentration camp, tells a remarkable story about how she and her sister Betsie were faced with the question of giving thanks in almost impossible situations.

As prisoners, the sisters were moved into new permanent barracks at Ravensbruck, Germany. The building where they were assigned was packed with dirty, sweat-stained prisoners: 1,400 were crammed into a space designed for 400. Plumbing had backed up; walls and floors were soiled and rancid. There were no individual beds, only rows of claustrophobic platforms to sleep on, precariously stacked three high and wedged side-by-side and end-to-end. Another misery would soon be discovered. Corrie wrote:

Suddenly I sat up, striking my head on the cross-slats above. Something had pinched my leg.

"Fleas," I cried. *"Betsie, the place is swarming with them!"*[1]

The sisters prayed, asking the Lord to show them how they could live in such a place. And then, with great silent words coming from the Lord Himself, the sisters were reminded of the Scripture they had read that morning from a Bible they kept hidden in a pouch around Corrie's neck. They were reminded to give thanks in all situations.

"That's it, Corrie," Betsie said. "That's His answer. 'Give thanks in all circumstances.' That's what we can do. We can start right now to thank God for every single thing about this new barracks!"

"Such as?" I said.

"Such as being assigned here together."

I bit my lip. "Oh yes, Lord Jesus!"

"Such as what you're holding in your hands." I looked down at the Bible.

"Yes! Thank You, dear Lord, that there was no inspection when we entered here!"

"Thank you," Betsie went on serenely in prayer, "for the fleas and for—"

The fleas! This was too much. "Betsie, there's no way even God can make me grateful for a flea."

"Give thanks in all circumstances," she quoted. "It doesn't say 'in pleasant circumstances.' Fleas are part of this place where God has put us."

And so we stood between tiers of bunks and gave thanks for fleas. But this time I was sure Betsie was wrong.[2]

Only later would the sisters realize how strategic fleas were to their situation. Each night the women held a Bible study in their barracks. At first Betsie and Corrie held the meetings with great timidity, fearing the guards. But as night after night went by and no guard ever came near, the sisters grew bolder. Soon, so many prisoners wanted to hear the message of the Gospel that the sisters held two services. There was constant supervision and harassment by the guards in other barracks, but in the Ten Booms' there was almost none. The sisters couldn't understand why.

Finally, they found out that it was the fleas! Guards would not step through their doorway for fear of fleas.

"My mind rushed back to our first hour in this place," Corrie writes. "I remembered Betsie's bowed head, and remembered her thanks to God for creatures I could see no use for."[3]

A Shocking Preposition

Go back with me to your high school English class for a moment and let's talk about prepositions. Wait, wait—keep reading. I won't put you to sleep, I promise. Remember prepositions? They're those little words or phrases that show the relationship of a noun to another noun—"at," "by," "for," "with," and so on.

How does a grammar lesson relate to thankfulness? One of these prepositions is absolutely shocking when we think about how the Lord uses it in Scripture to tell us how to cultivate grateful hearts.

The preposition is "for" and it's found in Ephesians 5:20: "always giving thanks to God the Father *for* everything, in the name of our Lord Jesus Christ" (emphasis added).

This verse, along with 1 Thessalonians 5:18 ("give thanks in all circumstances, for this is God's will for you in Christ Jesus"), forms the foundation for what I'm talking about in this book. These verses tell us that we're to give thanks at all times, everywhere, no matter what. The emphasis is on time—to give thanks always, continually, no matter if our circumstances are pleasant or horrific. *Always. Continually.* Let that sink in, my friend. When we think about it, that idea can be so shocking. How do you always give thanks *for* everything?!

That one little preposition puts such weight on things.

Let me explain what I mean. I want you to imagine the absolute worst thing you can think of in life. Perhaps it's rape, murder, starvation, or the death of a child. We live in a fallen world, and sin happens. It's part of what God allows His children to experience as part of His plan. Yet these verses tell us to give thanks *for* all things—to give thanks no matter what happens.

Is that tough to get a grip on? It is for me. God calls us to give thanks not only for our comforts but also for our afflictions.

That means we're to give thanks

- even if our child has died;
- even if we've been the victim of sexual molestation;
- even if there are fleas in our concentration camp barrack.

Wow. That is no easy thing to do. When God's Word is laid out for us like that, sometimes it's hard to grasp. Giving thanks in all situations is radical business. When God calls us to a task, He seldom calls us to an easy one. Giving thanks *for* all things is no exception.

Maybe right now you are walking through a time of extreme pain. If that is your experience, I do not take it lightly. Perhaps you've just experienced a sorrow that has torn your world in two. It may be tough right now to read these words in Scripture that tell you to give thanks in all things. Know that I'm praying for you and your circumstances, even as I write this book.

35

Yet please know that God is never a God of coldness or heartlessness. He doesn't look at us when we're going through troubling times and tell us to simply buck up or put a smiley face on our most heartbreaking situations. That's not what these verses mean at all. As we'll soon see in another verse, giving thanks always recognizes the greatness and compassion of a God who loves us so intently, so passionately, so wonderfully that words can barely express it. Giving thanks is part of God's design; when we look closely at this design, we can see something of the majesty of His

Being and of His care and concern for us—even in our most trying times.

God's Great Promise

God loves us. That's a promise.

How many times have you heard that He cares for you? It is true. He not only loves us but He also is in love with us. Scripture uses virtually every comparison possible to help us understand the love of Christ.

God loves us like a good father loves us (see 2 Thess. 2:16). Not everyone has grown up with a good father and can relate to this. But God is someone who is always there for us. He comforts, guides, cares for and protects us. He's the One who watches over us, who is tender toward us, who takes us in His arms and allows us to put our head on His shoulder. Have you ever seen a child at rest in her daddy's lap? This is a picture of God with us.

36

God loves us like a good husband (see Eph. 5:25). Not everyone has a good husband. Some people are single and have never experienced marriage. Some are divorced and wish they had married a good husband in the first place. But God's love for us is perfect. God is someone who loves us passionately. God encourages us and listens to us. He is all that we could hope for or imagine. Do you know, and can you picture, a husband and wife who clearly love each other? This is a picture of God with us.

God loves us like an amazing friend (see Jas. 2:23). Most of us can point to at least one good friend in our lives—someone who is patient and kind toward us, who is interested in us, believes in us, hopes in us. Who is your best friend? God is like this with us, only He does it perfectly.

God loves us, and when He calls us to give thanks always, He always does it out of love.

Romans 8:28 helps to put in perspective our call to give thanks in all circumstances: "And we know that in all things God works for the good of those who love him, who have been called according to his purpose." These words mean that all things we go through fit into God's plan—everything—even the most difficult experiences we go through. We may not know how or why we go through these things. We may never know. But we can trust the ways of a good God.

37

Whatever experiences you are going through right now, I invite you to run them through the words of Romans 8:28. This is not an invitation to add to Scripture, it's an invitation to make it personal. Try it with me. Fill in the blank below with a situation in your life that's on your mind and heart.

God causes all things, even _____

_____

_____

_____ *to work together for good.*

All things.

All things.

All things.

Somehow that little exercise always helps me to more clearly see my call to live a lifestyle of thanksgiving. To be thankful is to recognize God's control of our lives in every detail as He seeks to conform us to the image of His Son. It is because of Romans 8:28 that verses such as 1 Thessalonians 5:18 and Ephesians 5:20 make sense to us. We are able to thank the Lord continually because we know that all things fit into His plan. We can thank God *for* everything, because in all things God works together for our good.

I want to offer a caveat when it comes to giving thanks for all things. This is not a way of weaseling out of God's directive for our lives—not at all! We are to take the whole of Scripture and apply it to our lives. We must carefully look at a verse and apply it correctly, taking into consideration the whole counsel of God.

The preposition "for" in Ephesians 5:20 has a primary meaning of "over" in the original language. God is telling us to give thanks *over* every situation, or "in the midst of" or "through" something.

In Scripture, God has clearly identified certain things that He calls wrong. The Ten Commandments, for example, itemize what God clearly detests. God hates murder. He hates idolatry. He hates stealing. He hates immorality. Never in Scripture does God ask us to call good what He calls evil. When God calls sin "sin," His request of us is that we agree with Him. What God calls evil, we are to call evil as well.

So the caveat is this: When it comes to giving thanks for all things, God doesn't ask us to call "good" what He calls "evil."

Is murder good? No. God calls it evil, and we are to call it evil as well.

Is rape good? No. God calls it wrong, and we are to call it wrong as well.

Is starvation good? No. God calls it unjust, and we are to call it unjust as well.

So how do we give thanks for all things, even when God clearly calls some things wrong?

I invite you to go back to the text and see what God's Word says. Give thanks *over* all things, or through all things, or in the midst of all things. Yes, always give thanks *for* all things, because all things fit into the Lord's perfect plan. All things themselves may not be good, but God harmonizes them together for the believer's ultimate benefit. And that's the context for always giving thanks.

In this manner, Corrie and Betsie ten Boom could thank the Lord continually, even in the midst of a situation that God called evil. Were the horrors of the Nazi concentration camps wrong? Absolutely. Did God ask Corrie and Betsie to call "good" what He calls "evil"? No.

But He still called them to give thanks.

Everywhere.

No matter what the circumstances.

In everything, give thanks.

Even for fleas.

Our God of Wonders

Giving thanks for all things can be done, even when times are hard. I've seen examples of this in the attitudes of the people closest to me.

My mother, for example, had a tremendous influence on my life, not only because of what she said, but also because of who she was. After my dad died in 1976, my mom had a habit of asking God every morning when she woke up, "Lord, what wonderful things do you have for me today?" I watched my mom, who had never worked a day outside of her home, who had never paid a bill or balanced a checkbook before my dad died, transfer the responsibility for her total care to her Father God—the God who loved her more than she could imagine. That's one way of giving thanks in all things: practicing dependence on the Lord daily. My mom had learned to trust God closely after years of walking with Him. She knew that God is a good and gracious God and that she was living out the plan God had for her, even though she was now a widow. My mom knew that God could be trusted.

My mom's example helped me learn how to be thankful for everything that comes my way, both the good and the bad. I can say without a doubt that God has taken care of me all the years since I asked Jesus into my heart as a twelve-year-old girl. He helped me even during the years that I tried to run my own life. His mercy and grace are greater than all the sins of the world put together. God has taught me that His way is always best, His plans always work and His love is unfailing.

If we learn to practice a lifestyle of thankfulness, it will transform our lives and help us walk in victory every day. As we learn to praise God for who He is and thank Him for what He does, we open our hearts completely to Him.

Friends, you can do it. You can cultivate a lifestyle of thankfulness, no matter what your situation. My prayer is that you will become more and more aware of God's love and concern for you, whatever you are going through right now. I pray that your roots will continue to go deep in Christ and that you will become strong and courageous as you learn to trust Him with everything life brings.

41

Prayer

Dear Lord, teach me to cultivate a thankful
heart as a gift to You and to the world around me.
Remind me when I grumble and complain that
Your will for me is to speak blessings and to be
a blessing to everyone I know. Amen.

Notes

1. Corrie ten Boom and John and Elizabeth Sherrill, *The Hiding Place* (Uhrichsville, OH: Barbour Publishing, 1971), n.p.
2. Ibid., n.p.
3. Ibid., n.p.

The Power of Thanks

Praise the LORD, O my soul, and forget not all his benefits.
PSALM 103:2

Have you ever thought about what strong connections there are between thanking God, worshiping God, and our health? Think about it: When we thank God, we agree with His plan—we are calling His purposes good and we're acknowledging that He is in control. That's worship, my friend. When we thank God, we are calling Him great and we are walking in the paths that He has set for us.

There is tremendous power for our daily living when we adopt this mind-set. God is the fountain of all that is good, and when we thank Him, no matter what we are going through, our hearts and spirits are lifted out of the trappings of lesser things. When we thank God, we set our minds on things above. God is great and worthy to be praised. God is to be worshiped because He is the great King.

Worshiping God through gratitude is simply a healthy thing to do. As we talked about in previous chapters, our minds and our bodies are connected. If we go around all day thinking negative thoughts, our bodies can be negatively affected. The opposite is true as well. If our daily thoughts are filled with positive things, our thoughts can positively affect our bodies.

I want to be careful how I say this, because worshiping God through gratitude is not just a magic pill that makes us feel better. That concept cheapens God, and frankly, it isn't true. We worship God simply because He is worthy to be worshiped—end of story. What I'm saying is this: When we sincerely worship God—when we fill our minds with His greatness and goodness and we filter all our experiences through His loving and guiding plan—there is also a side benefit for us. When we worship God, we know what is really true in life. And that's a healthy perspective for us to have.

Wisdom from the Psalms

43

Look with me for a moment at one of my favorite portions of Scripture, Psalm 103:1-5:

> Praise the LORD, O my soul; all my inmost being, praise his holy name. Praise the LORD, O my soul, and forget not all his benefits—who forgives all your sins and heals all your diseases, who redeems your life from the pit and crowns you with love and compassion, who satisfies your desires with good things so that your youth is renewed like the eagle's.

These verses express beautifully the reasons that I believe God wants us to be thankful. When we're thankful, we agree with God. When we're thankful, we praise His name. Being thankful puts sorrow in perspective. It's an antidote to bitterness, anger and despair. When we're thankful, we find hope in our relationship with Christ. He has a plan for our lives, and when we're thankful, we agree with His plan.

This is a powerful way of living. Think about it. Circumstances can rock our world. Our level of happiness can go up and down like a yo-yo when we allow our happiness to depend upon what we go through. But we can have tremendous confidence for daily living when we adopt the consistent mind-set of thanksgiving.

Let's look at the power of thanks God offers in the above Psalm. When we praise God with all our inmost being, it sets our hearts and minds on God's plan, not ours. God's plan is good—that alone is reason enough to be thankful. Walk with me through each main phrase of these verses.

He Forgives All My Sins

A friend of mine has said many times while teaching, "The Greek word for 'all' is 'ALL.'" When I think about having a God big enough and powerful enough to forgive all my sins, I am flooded with thankfulness. Sometimes when we sin, we can get so wrapped up in self-hate afterwards. Yet 1 John 1:9 says that if we confess our sin, He is faithful and just to forgive. Forgiveness and cleansing is part of God's plan. There is power when we remember this and when we thank God for His great ability to forgive.

I will never forget a Sunday morning many years ago. There I was, a 12-year-old girl, sitting in Sunday School. Our church was having what we called revival meetings, and the visiting evangelist, Bo Baker, was the speaker in my class that morning. Bo started out by sharing a passage from Matthew 24 that talks about the second coming of Christ. In this chapter, Jesus says that when He returns to take all believers in Him back to heaven, people will be doing pretty much what they have always been doing. They will still be eating and drinking, marrying and going on about their daily life. Jesus says the only difference on that momentous day from any other day is that some of those people will be taken to heaven with Him and some will be left behind. Tim LaHaye and Jerry Jenkins did a masterful job of depicting this scene in the Left Behind book series they wrote.

Bo Baker asked the group of 12-year-old boys and girls sitting around me that morning, "Do you know which group you will be in when Jesus comes again?" Immediately in my heart I knew that I would be in the group left behind. So when Bo invited us to pray and ask Jesus to come into our hearts, I did just that. That morning, I received Jesus' forgiveness for every sin I had ever committed, and He gave me a new heart in place of the one with which I was born.

I am still thankful today for that morning and for the forgiveness I experienced, but the tremendous benefit of becoming a Christian is that God continues to forgive all my sins. How I wish the list of bad things I have done was only as long as the list committed by the 12-year-old girl that morning. All believers in Christ come to realize that we will sin and continue to sin as long as we have life in our bodies. The great benefit of knowing Christ personally is that every time I come to Him and confess that I have messed up one more time, He forgives me again, again and again. This first benefit is a huge one and a great reason to be thankful.

He heals All My Diseases

Another benefit of being a Christian is that every disease you or I experience in this life is assured of healing—if not in this life, then in the life to come. Have you ever stopped to think about the benefit of healing? The common cold can make us miserable, but after about seven days our noses dry up and we quit sneezing and coughing. A deep cut in our finger will heal and be as good as new before long. Our bodies are miraculous in their innate ability to heal, but ultimately they will give out and break down.

My friend, Cheri Lasiter, was born with cerebral palsy. Life is a struggle for her every day. She walks with a walker and has constant pain in her back. Despite her physical difficulties, Cheri told me that she is thankful for her disability. I asked Cheri one day after a First Place weight-loss class how she could possibly be thankful for cerebral palsy. She shared with me how her disease had slowed her down and helped her meet many wonderful people. From her drivers to the friends she has made in church and First Place, Cheri feels blessed.

With all the difficulties in Cheri's life, she has grabbed hold of what is important. Everyone in our class is inspired by Cheri's tenacity and her determination to never give up. Has God healed her cerebral palsy? No, but He has given Cheri abundant life in the midst of it. Ultimate healing probably won't come to Cheri until she leaves this earthly body. But God has healed her emotions, her soul and her mind.

How can we complain about minor aches and pains when others around us are able to be thankful for major illnesses and disabilities? Yes, another benefit of knowing Christ is that He heals all our diseases. Nineteenth-century preacher and theologian Charles Haddon Spurgeon said, "The Lord gets His best soldiers out of the highlands of affliction."[1]

He Redeems My Life from the Pit

All of us have gone through "pit" experiences. My friend Duane Miller had a life-changing pit experience. Duane was pastor of First Baptist Church in Brenham, Texas, when suddenly he started losing his ability to speak. After a while, he was forced to resign as pastor and move back to Houston. He was out of a job, and things didn't look good.

Duane was originally a member of First Baptist Houston, where I serve, and his friends here went to

Brenham and retrieved Duane and his family. They brought them back to Houston, and Duane started teaching a large Bible study class at church. The doctors warned Duane that if he continued using his voice, one day before very long he would never be able to speak again. Things went from bad to worse in Duane's personal life, and on the Sunday morning that Duane was speaking from this very passage in the Psalms, his life was in the pit. He had exhausted his last opportunity for employment, because he could not speak. He felt worthless and had asked God the day before to take him home.

Duane had a special microphone to speak. When he taught, his voice was less than pleasant to hear. It sounded gravelly, and he spoke every word with great difficulty. Nevertheless, his class loved his teaching and insisted that he remain as teacher of the class.

This particular morning when Duane began teaching, he was reading from Psalm 103. As he read verses 1 to 5, his voice began to return. By the time he got to the part "he redeems my life from the pit," the gravelly sound began to change. The lesson was taped that morning, and you could hear people beginning to weep. Some were loudly thanking and praising God for what they were witnessing, because that morning, after three long years, Duane Miller's life was redeemed from the pit.

Yes, this was a miraculous healing for Duane; but the reality is that God also wants to redeem our lives from the pit. Can we learn to thank God for our pit experiences? Can we trust Him to redeem our lives? Duane says that although he was as low as he could get and had never been thankful for his own pit experience, God still had a plan that included redeeming his life. I know that today, Duane is eternally grateful for his pit experience, because it has given him hundreds of opportunities to share how our God redeems our lives from the pit. Duane has told his story all over the world since that day and many have been blessed by his story of God's miraculous healing.

He Crowns Me with Love and Compassion

49

This morning, as I was driving into work, I was thanking God for His tremendous love and compassion for me. I was struck by how hard it has been to write my last two books. As I thought back, I realized that when I wrote *Today Is the First Day,* it was just six weeks after the death of our daughter Shari. I had nothing in me to write those 90 devotionals, but God had much to say. He took over, and in His love and compassion, He used my brain and my hands and helped me write every word. The same thing happened with *Back on Track.* I was at a low point physically, following injuries, surgery and weight gain. God held my hand as I believed, trusted and obeyed Him while writing the book. I can honestly say that *Back on Track* was very easy to write.

When my granddaughter Cara and I wrote *The Mother-Daughter Legacy*, it was a book of healing and therapy for both of us because of the recent loss of my mom and my daughter Shari, and the loss of Cara's mom (Shari). It was also a tribute to the legacy they had passed to us, so it was an easy book to write.

As I was thinking about the ease with which I had written the last three previously mentioned books, I wondered why I had experienced such difficulty writing *The Divine Diet* and now this book on thankfulness. I was bowled over to realize that I have been relatively trauma-free while writing the last two books and have not depended on God for every word that I write. I immediately asked His forgiveness and thanked Him for His love and compassion toward me, asking Him to finish the writing of this book and to once again use my brain and hands to do it. Yes, God's love and compassion for His children are benefits we cannot take for granted.

He Satisfies My Desires with Good Things

Food does a great job of satisfying my physical and emotional desires, but the food I eat doesn't always bring good things into my life. When I make bad choices in food, I gain weight and feel badly about myself. One of the benefits of being a Christian is that God satisfies all my desires with good things.

The Bible tells us to "delight yourself in the LORD and he will give you the desires of your heart" (Psalm 37:4). In the last 15 years, since I gave God permission to be the boss of my entire life—not just boss of certain areas I chose to give Him—I can honestly say that He has satisfied every desire He has placed in my heart. He has lavished His love on Johnny and me in the midst of some of the most difficult circumstances of our entire married life. For example, He gave us our home on Galveston Bay, a place we had always loved. Our home is just five streets away from the bay home my parents owned and where our children spent many carefree years as kids. What better place for Johnny, who has cancer, to be. The air is cleaner than Houston air, the scenery is gorgeous and life is slow-paced and serene.

God has fulfilled desires that I had for years and some desires that I never had. One of my desires was to have a First Place F.O.C.U.S. (Focusing On Christ's Unlimited Strength) Week where men and women could experience a spa-like experience for a week, which would include spiritual and emotional nourishment in addition to the physical experience. This dream has become a reality, and last year we reached our capacity several months before the October event.

51

I had never dreamed of writing a book. The first book I wrote, *Choosing to Change,* was only because I knew that someone needed to chronicle the First Place story. I also knew that Dottie Brewer, founder of the First Place program, would be more than a little upset with me when I got to heaven if I had failed to tell the world about the humble beginnings of the program. God wanted this book, and He went so far as to wake me in the middle of the night to give me the title of the book and the title of all the chapters. I wrote this book by speaking it into a tape recorder. My daughter-in-law, Lisa, transcribed every word into print. From that first book, written strictly out of obedience to God's leading, He has blessed me with seven more books in print.

So you see, God satisfies our every desire, whether known or unknown, with good things. The place where I live is satisfying an immediate desire for me, while the books I write satisfies His desires for my life.

The Power of Thanks

How good it is for us to give thanks! Whatever your need today—whether physical, mental, emotional or spiritual—God is with you. True thankfulness springs from hearts that know that everything we have and everything we are comes from our creator God. When we give thanks to God, we worship Him.

In the chapters ahead, we are going to look at specific areas of life in which we can give thanks. You will read real stories about real people who have experienced some of life's most common situations and have survived these difficult trials.

It is my prayer that as you read the rest of this book, God will continue to teach you about Himself and why a thankful heart will not only change you but will also change your circumstances. Each of us has the opportunity to choose thankfulness in every situation.

As we look at what true thankfulness is and why we should practice thankfulness as a powerful part of daily life, I believe that God will reveal Himself to us in ways we never dreamed possible.

Prayer

Dear Father, I want to thank You right now that You have forgiven every sin I have ever committed and every sin I will ever commit. Thank You that this was made possible because Jesus was willing to die on the cross, not only for my sins, but also for the sins of the entire world. Thank You for all the benefits that come because I have accepted Your free gift of salvation. Help me cultivate a heart that is truly thankful, not only for all You do, but also for Who You are. Amen.

53

Note

1. Charles Haddon Spurgeon, *Gleanings Among the Sheaves* (Grand Rapids, MI: Baker Books, 1988), n.p.

CHAPTER 5

Thankful for Difficult People

If anyone says, "I love God," yet hates his brother, he is a liar.

1 JOHN 4:20

We hardly ever put the people in our lives into categories by speaking those categories. Do you know what I mean? Seldom ever do we actually say out loud, "That person is so-o-o-o difficult!" It's usually what we whisper or what we think in our hearts but don't say. If you and I could scream from the highest mountaintop our true feelings about all the people in our lives over the past few years, what would we hear?

Hike with me up to the top of a mountain peak for a moment. Are you ready for a shout? Don't worry; no one will hear you except the wind and the trees. Ready? Do you have a person in your life that you would undeniably categorize as difficult? Shout out that person's name now:

_____!!!

Maybe you shouted the name of the 110-year-old clerk at the grocery store whose line you try to avoid because she always greets you with a sneer.

Maybe you shouted your sister-in-law's name. She always manages to weave her longstanding belief that no one has ever been good enough for her brother into every conversation with you.

Maybe you shouted your next-door-neighbors' names. They're not married, but they live together—which you've always found hard to accept. They're also noisy and they never mow their lawn. To top it off, the trash cans in front of their house always look gross.

Maybe you shouted the name of your supervisor at work. If only she (or he) would see your way of thinking once in a while.

Maybe you shouted your kids' names or your mom's or the pastor of your church . . . or your husband's.

Maybe you shouted a whole list of names.

Maybe you're still shouting!

I could point to several people I have known and interacted with over the years whom I would categorize as difficult. It's a fact that people have different opinions; they come from different perspectives, and not everybody is nice or gracious. Sure, sometimes there are obvious reasons why people are difficult. Maybe they're as angry as snarling dogs or as conniving and sly as serpents, talking bad behind your back or cutting you down when you're not looking. Sometimes the reasons are less obvious. Maybe the person you're thinking of had a poor upbringing. Or maybe he or she is just sad or lonely. When people have been deeply hurt in their lives, one of the responses they can choose is to hurt back. Difficult people exist wherever you go.

It's okay to acknowledge that someone in your life is not easy to get along with. Jesus encountered difficult people all the time. He got so angry with the moneychangers in the Temple that He physically threw them out (see John 2:13-17). The people in His own hometown refused to honor Him (see Matt. 13:53-58). The Pharisees criticized Him for being friends with all the wrong people (see Mark 7:1-6). His disciples squabbled in His presence over who would be greatest (see Luke 9:46).

Martha scolded Him.

Thomas doubted Him.

Peter denied Him.

Judas betrayed Him.

And these were some of His closest friends. If we have difficult people in our lives, we are in good company. Welcome to the real world of relationships.

I don't believe we will ever avoid difficult relationships. They are here to stay. Usually, when I repeatedly come in contact with a difficult person, there is a lesson I need to learn. Until I am willing to learn it, the situation will repeat itself over and over. This is why we can't run from the difficult people in our lives. Changing jobs is not the answer, because there will be difficult people at the next job. Moving to a new home is not the answer, because there will be a new neighbor who is also difficult.

Could it be that God places difficult people in our lives for a reason?

A Hard Prayer to Pray

God, thank you for the difficult people in my life.

Can you honestly pray that prayer?

It's not always easy, is it? Most of us have no trouble thanking God for the people in our lives who are easy to love. Yet being thankful for those people who are hard to love is difficult to grasp and even more difficult to practice.

Friends, being thankful for the difficult people in our lives is a huge part of the solution. As we learn to thank God for the people who give us the most problems, we let go of the problems and allow God to begin working, not only in our life but in the life of the other person as well.

When we encounter difficult people, what can we thank God for?

To begin with, we can thank the Lord that this person is part of His plan. Instead of our running from the difficult people in our life, God desires to change us first as we learn how to thank Him for our difficult person. It has been my experience that after I've learned the lesson God has for me, He either heals the other person or He moves them on to some other place. In either case, I am better off as I learn to love the difficult people in my life. Ultimately, I believe that God uses difficult people in my life as sandpaper to heal my own character flaws and continue to transform me into the image of His Son.

Giving thanks for difficult people also demonstrates the type of love God has for us. God is all about demonstrating unconditional love. He loves people not because of what they do or what they have but simply because they exist. In Romans 5:8, God tells us that

He loves us in this way: "While we were still sinners, Christ died for us." This is the type of love God calls us to have for other people. It's a type of love that illustrates God's grace.

When it comes to thanking God for the difficult people in my life, there's a Scripture verse that I find particularly powerful. It is 1 John 4:20: "If anyone says, 'I love God,' yet hates his brother, he is a liar. For anyone who does not love his brother, whom he has seen, cannot love God, whom he has not seen." This means that God has intertwined two kinds of love: love for Him and love for others. We cannot have one without the other. Our love for God can be best seen in our love for people. If we don't love others, we don't love God. Those are strong words.

I believe that thanking God for the person who gives us the greatest difficulty teaches our hearts about the great love God has for people. Thankfulness works a miracle in our hearts and changes our attitude about that difficult person.

It has been my experience that people don't enjoy being difficult, even though it sometimes seems that way. People are usually difficult because of some unhealed hurt in their heart. This hurt causes them to lash out at others, which in turn causes others to avoid them like the plague. A cycle begins that can only be broken when a child of God decides to break the cycle.

Friends, we have been given that call.

Denise's Story

It can be hard to thank God for difficult people. Yet God calls us to do this. Denise Munton, who wrote our First Place Bible study *Living in Grace* tells a story that perfectly illustrates this truth. Denise writes:

> In my life was a person who hurt me deeply, even from the beginning of our relationship. She held very high expectations for everyone in her world. I never felt that I could please her. The relationship was one that I couldn't discard or avoid, considering my circumstances.
>
> For years, I lived in fear and dread whenever I was around her. I had an opportunity at one point to confront the situation and share my feelings, but she refused to allow that to happen. I, in turn, became very resentful and angry. My bitterness began to affect my relationship with my husband. I even blamed her for the conflict it was causing in my marriage.
>
> I had the privilege to sit down and receive counsel from Gary Smalley about my situation, as his daughter, Kari, and I are close friends. Kari and I sat down with Dr. Smalley together, picking his brain, thinking he would be able to advise me on what I needed to "do." I was ready to tackle this situation and resolve it with this person whether she wanted to or not.

To my surprise, all Dr. Smalley counseled me to do was to be thankful. He told me to pray and thank the Lord for this situation and for that person because of how it has caused me to have to depend in a greater way on Him, and because it is unwise to confront someone who is unwilling to listen and work through the difficulty.

Give thanks. That was his advice. It took me a while but I finally yielded to the Lord and asked Him for help. Though I wanted to confront my difficult friend and let her know how badly she hurt me, I knew that I was only to pray for her. I even began my prayers with "God, I don't feel like praying for her. I've been hurt so badly. Help me. Okay, I thank you for her."

I began thanking God for this person each day. Soon, I was past telling God that I didn't want to pray for her, and I began to see her through His eyes. I began to feel compassion for her. I began to pray for her using sections of God's Word as a guide. I would pray for her to be free from her own heartaches.

Soon, my whole heart and attitude toward her began to change. I was experiencing freedom. I wasn't fearful of her anymore; and if she was rude or demanding, I wasn't noticing. I found that my heart softened. I would choose to not allow her attitude and actions control my attitude and actions. Instead, I began over-looking her attitude. These were supernatural responses, I realize now, as I walked obediently in Christ. Nothing in me wanted to love her, yet Christ gave me the ability to do so. By thanking God for this person, I found that I felt free.

It was a few years before I began to see a change in my friend's heart. It wasn't that I was waiting and watching for God to change her. In fact, I really didn't expect it. But, over the years, I truly began to see her soften. As I was obedient to Christ to express thankfulness for her, God had changed my heart and perspective in the relationship and I was free to extend grace. God, then, was faithful to do a work in that person, His child, like He was doing in me.

61

The Power of Unconditional Thanks

As we thank God for our difficult person, God begins to place His unconditional love for that person in our heart. God's love has the miracle-working power to change the life of any difficult person. The most difficult person in the world cannot resist the unconditional love of God when it is practiced day after day in the midst of the difficulty. First Thessalonians 5:15 says, "Make sure that nobody pays back wrong for wrong, but always try to be kind to each other and to everyone else."

I have worked with many difficult people over the last 30 years, but I can honestly say that not one of them was really a bad person. In fact, most of the difficult people I have worked with have been Christians. It has been said that the Christian army is the only army in the world that shoots its wounded. Most difficult people are wounded warriors in the battle of life. Our unconditional love for the difficult people God places in our life has the power to heal their hearts and thus allow them to change for the better. And it accomplishes a miracle in us as well.

Prayer

Dear Lord, I know you are aware of how hard it is for me to thank you for (let alone love)

_____.

I am going to do my part by thanking You for creating _____ and placing him/her in my life. Thank you for loving _____ and for loving me as well when I am difficult. Please use me as an instrument of change in _____'s life as you teach me to love him/her. Amen.

Money Solutions

[Do not] put [your] hope in wealth, which is so uncertain, but put [your] hope in God, who richly provides us with everything for our enjoyment.

1 TIMOTHY 6:17

In 1959, when Johnny and I married, money wasn't a huge concern to us. We didn't have much of it, but it also didn't seem to take a lot of money to live back then.

The first year of our marriage, Johnny was in college and worked part-time, so we lived with my parents. After that year, Johnny surprised me with $1,000 he had been able to save, and we purchased our first home in the summer of 1960. I am amazed today to think about the low cost of living in those days. Our first home had a living room, dining room, kitchen, three bedrooms, one bath, hardwood floors and an attached one-car garage, all for the price of $10,700 and a monthly payment of $72! A week's worth of groceries could be purchased for $10 and provided enough food to fill four paper grocery bags. Johnny brought home $116 a week, so it never seemed like we struggled to make ends meet.

By our fifth anniversary, we had three children under age four. Even then, money didn't seem to be a huge problem. Yet unbeknownst to us, we had developed some poor habits related to how we thought of and handled money. Everything we brought in, we spent. Whatever we desired, we bought on credit. We saved nothing and gave little to our church. Our financial lifestyle was a prescription for financial disaster, but we didn't realize how much trouble we were in.

We continued to live in this manner until 1979. For 15 years, Johnny sold forklifts for a large company in Houston and made enough money to take good care of our family. We didn't consider ourselves rich, but truthfully, we were very comfortable. In 1979, Johnny opened his own forklift company, and things went well for a couple of years. In the early 1980s, the Houston economy nose-dived, and almost everyone began to struggle financially. Mortgage rates soared to 18 percent, and companies were going under every day. We were no exception. The forklift business in Houston dried up almost overnight and Johnny's business quickly went through financial ruin. We struggled to keep the business afloat until 1984, when we were forced to shut the doors and close it down.

We were broke.

Our two daughters, Lisa and Shari, married in 1980 and 1981, and for a while our son, John, was the only one still at home. John graduated from high school in 1982 and received a baseball scholarship to Southwestern University in Georgetown, Texas. Even with his scholarship, we still owed $12,000 for his freshman year. It took everything we could scrape together to make it through the first year. After the end of the school year, we were forced to bring John home, and he worked and put himself through college.

By 1984, we had lost everything except our home and furnishings. We didn't have a business; we didn't have a job; we didn't even have our cars. Johnny had been forced to refinance our vehicles to keep the business going. Some dear friends, Don and Sarah Hunt, took pity on us and hired us to work at their stone yard. They paid us well; Johnny started selling ornamental stone and I did the payroll and kept the books. We lived this way for a few months. But when we were honest with ourselves, we knew we were both pretty miserable. I had left a 12-year ministry job at our church to help Johnny in his forklift business before it failed. I had loved working at the church. The irony (and Johnny and I both laugh about it today) is that I might have actually contributed to the downfall of Johnny's business, even after leaving my church job. I just didn't have the same passion Johnny had for forklifts. I spent my time going to lunch with friends and handling the company's books the way we handled our home finances.

How could we ever be thankful in the midst of this mess?

I will never forget the words Johnny said to me one Friday after we returned home from work at the stone yard. He said, "Carole, you're miserable. I want you to call First Baptist Church and take any job they have available." He knew that I had felt dejected since I left full-time ministry. He assured me that even if I had to take a salary cut, we would make it. Ministry was where my heart was and where I believed God had called me to be. The next Monday morning, August 15, 1984, I made the call to the church and immediately took a job as receptionist in the education department of the church. (I still work at that church today!)

Initially, I took a $500 a month cut in salary from what I was paid at the stone yard. But within six weeks, I had been promoted and was receiving the same salary as I had received at my previous job. Even though God had used my husband to position me back at First Baptist, Johnny and I were still in dire financial straits. We thought we were flat broke, but we were about to get "broker" still. In the summer of 1984, we were forced to file for bankruptcy—jobs and all. It was the bleakest time of our marriage—spiritually, emotionally, mentally and financially.

Thank You, Lord, Even Through This

How could I ever give thanks in the midst of our financial hardship?

My journey toward gratitude began with Pat Lewis, one of my dearest friends in the world. Pat and I have been friends for more than 35 years. God knew she was probably the only person in the world to whom I would listen about truth, thankfulness, money and

God's plan for my life. Pat told me later that she didn't want to do this, but God had begun gently speaking to her heart about talking to me. For three weeks, God spoke to her through every sermon or Christian radio program she heard. She knew what needed to be done.

Pat and I had a tradition of Christmas shopping together every December. I use the term "shopping" loosely, because we seldom bought anything on our day together. We'd meet early for breakfast, shop until lunch, have a bite, shop till dinner, and then dine together. It was always just a day of being with each other as friends.

Pat was working at First Baptist at the time. She would pick me up every morning and drive me home after work. Because of her love and loyalty to me, God used Pat to speak His words to my heart at the end of our day of Christmas shopping. When we returned to my house, we had been sitting outside visiting for a few moments when she said there was something we need-ed to discuss. She told me she believed that God want-ed to do something really big in my life and her fear was that I might miss it if I didn't give up control of my life to Him.

67

Control? What did that have to do with anything? Johnny and I were broke and in debt up to our eyelids. If anything, we needed to strike oil.

Pat's words began to sink in. I knew that I was completely destitute in every area of life but didn't know where to begin to make a change, so I did what is so easy to do in those situations—I sat in the car and cried. Pat cried with me, and we prayed together before I went inside. Pat is a very serious individual, so I didn't take lightly what she had shared with me. For two weeks, I pondered everything she had said on that momentous night.

Two weeks after our talk, I sat in church on a Sunday morning, listening to my pastor, Dr. John Bisagno. He spoke about how God is a perfect gentleman when it comes to our will. God seldom works on our stubbornness without first receiving our permission. Dr. Bisagno told us that if we were not willing for God to do the work needed, we could pray this prayer: "Lord, I am not willing, but I am willing to be made willing." He said this prayer gives God permission to start the needed work in our lives to break our stubborn will. As sincerely as I have ever prayed, I prayed the prayer that very morning and closed it with "and please don't let it hurt too bad!"

68

I just knew this was going to be the most awful experience of my life; but God knew this was the low point I had to get to for Him to get my attention.

I surrendered all to Christ.

From that day forward, everything started changing for the better. Was I thankful at the time for the financial straits our family was in? Of course not! I was a carnal Christian who had refused to give God control of my life. I accepted Christ at the age of 12 but had pretty much run my life my way since that time and until it was totally shipwrecked.

Am I thankful today for how God fixed the financial mess we had made? Oh, yes, yes, and again, *yes!* Our God gives exceedingly, abundantly over all we can ever ask or think (see Eph. 3:20).

When I think of all the ways that God has prospered us financially since then, I am more amazed than anyone else. In 1987, He took me, with only a high school education, and gave me the job of directing the First Place program, just three short years after He took over the reins of my life. I can honestly say that God has done it all; my job has been to hang on for the ride.

When the Lord Takes Over

69

Right now you may be struggling financially as we were at one time. Please know that our God owns the cattle on a thousand hills. He has the resources to fix whatever problem you may have. If you're asking yourself, *How can I ever thank God for what I'm going through?* let me tell you that I know it's not easy. But He cares about what concerns you, and He is in control.

In my own life, financial problems were the tools God used to bring me to the end of myself so that He could remake me into the woman He had always wanted me to be. I am forever grateful for our money woes, because they were the vehicle that drove me to God.

I don't know the specific ways that God will work in your life. I can only offer my testimony at this point. My aim in talking honestly and transparently about my family's financial struggles is to encourage you that God can and will get you out of any money pit you may be in if you will hand over the reins of your life to Him. Here are some of the things God did after He took over control of my life.

Credit Rating

Our credit rating was not the greatest before our financial ruin, simply because of sloppy bill paying. I didn't see the importance of paying our bills on time. More than once we had the lights or water turned off because I had misplaced a bill and forgotten to pay it. This was during the years that we had enough money to pay our bills. Imagine how hard it was to restore our shattered credit rating after bankruptcy. When God took over, He gave us the desire to change and to repay the mountain of credit-card debt we had accrued. Today, we are grateful to God for an excellent credit rating, due in great measure to our obedience and God's great mercy and grace in our lives.

Debt

As God began to take over financially, we eventually got out of debt. This did not happen overnight, because we had not gotten into this shape overnight. I believe the key to becoming debt-free is that we finally learned to live within our means.

Little by little, as we paid what we could, we got out of debt. Today, our only large payment is our house mortgage. We learned not to buy on credit if we could not pay for the purchase in full the next month. We pay every bill monthly when it arrives, but most of our bills are set up so that the full amount is deducted from our checking account each month on the due date. Twenty years ago, I never would have believed what God could accomplish by giving Him control of our finances. I certainly believe it today!

Tithing

Johnny and I had never consistently given 10 percent of our income back to God. (When you spend everything you make, there never seems to be enough left over for God.) But at the height of our money woes, we made the conscious decision to trust God fully and to give back to Him 10 percent of whatever He gave us.

71

I will be forever grateful for all that God taught me about giving back to Him what He already owns. The lesson is that when you don't have much money, it's easier to give back to Him than when you have a lot of money. Think about it—10 percent of $100 is $10; 10 percent of $1,000 is $100. Which seems easier to give— $10 or $100? The point is that you can't wait until you get more money before you start to tithe. At that point, the habit will not have been established, and your tithe will probably seem like too much to you then. The time to start tithing is now—even if you are in the midst of financial crisis. I am so thankful that He taught us to give to Him first before we paid any of our bills. When we trusted God with the 90 percent that was left, He miraculously took over our finances.

Savings

God has worked miracle after miracle to take care of our financial needs. Saving money was something we didn't start doing until 1987. I was 45 years old and Johnny was 47. We had lived our lives until then as though we would never get old! God sent people into our lives to give us guidance on how to save for retirement. Through that expert guidance and God's leadership, we learned how to save money before we ever got our hands on it. Today, money is deducted from my paycheck and invested in our Baptist Convention's Annuity Fund each month. Over time, it has grown into a nice little nest egg.

Financial Stability and God's Timing

God has done so much for us financially that I could write about it for days. One of the most amazing ways that He directed our lives happened in the summer of 1997. I wouldn't know until later how the Lord would use this situation, but it has all worked out in His perfect plan.

My associate, Kay Smith, and I taught two First Place Fitness Weeks that summer—one at LifeWay Christian Resource's Glorieta conference center in New Mexico, and the other at its Ridgecrest conference center in North Carolina. It was strange, but Johnny began talking to me every day that I was away about a crazy idea that had suddenly popped into his head.

During our daily phone call, all he could talk about was buying a second home on Galveston Bay. With me gone at the conference, he would drive down to the Bay, sit on the patio of whatever home was for sale and talk to me when I called that evening about how we needed to buy it. I couldn't imagine how we would ever be able to enjoy a second home with all the traveling I do. Because of Johnny's obvious excitement and his pressing me into action every time we talked on the phone, I got the feeling that wives get when we know the new car is going to be purchased whether we like it or not! I was so concerned that I even asked our participants at the Fitness Week to pray that if we had to buy a Bay house, it would be one we could afford.

73

The idea stayed in Johnny's mind. I still had apprehensions, but I wanted to support Johnny. So after I returned home that summer, we began hunting for a house on Galveston Bay together. On Labor Day weekend, a friend of Johnny's called to tell us about a house for sale at the Bay. His friend told him the cost and that this house already had a rental clientele. When we drove up to the house, we knew why it hadn't sold yet. It was the color of Pepto Bismol! Johnny didn't even want to go inside. Surely this could not be the house he had felt so pressed to purchase. We crept through the gate and walked out on the pier. It looked better from the water than it did from the street, but it still wasn't much.

The house was small, less than 1,000 square feet. We bought it in September 1997. Little did we know that a month later, Johnny would be diagnosed with stage four prostate cancer. Three days after his diagnosis, our son's home would burn to the ground, leaving John, his wife, Lisa, and their three children with just the clothes they were wearing.

John and his family moved into our Houston home after the fire, and we retreated to our little house at the Bay to grieve Johnny's diagnosis. We lived in that little house for two years until my mom moved in with us when she was no longer able to live alone.

God's plan and perfect timing for us was still being worked out. I had knee surgery in the fall of 1999 and couldn't walk during the weekend after the surgery.

To get me out of the house, Johnny took me for a ride in our golf cart around our neighborhood at the Bay. We went on a longer ride than usual and ended up on a street two miles over from our little house. We saw a house that looked fantastic, right on the water as we had always dreamed, and there just happened to be a For Sale By Owner sign hanging on its fence. Since we didn't have a pen, Johnny and I memorized the phone number on the sign so that we could call when we got back home.

We had tried to purchase several larger houses during the two years of living on the water, but God protected us each time, because He knew the timing wasn't yet right. Now that my mom was living with us full time and we really needed more room, God picked out the perfect house for us.

Just before we found that house, we had recently sold our home in Houston to the state of Texas so that Interstate 10 could be widened. Our son, John, and his family were able to live in that home for almost two years while they rebuilt their own home. God had taken care of absolutely every detail for all of us.

I am so thankful to God that He impressed on my sweet husband's heart that we needed to buy a second house at the Bay in the summer of 1997. If we had not purchased the house at the exact time we did, John and his family would have been hard-pressed to find a home to live in after their fire, and we would have missed these last seven years of bliss, living in our home on Galveston Bay.

75

God's Provision: Always Enough

My testimony about finances is this: God provides. He provides in His time and in His way, yet He always provides. God's provision is something worth reminding yourself of if you are struggling financially. The Lord is intimately acquainted with every detail of your life, including your finances. He knows what you are going through, and He knows what you need. Can you give Him thanks today that your current finances are part of His perfect plan for your life?

Johnny and I are supremely grateful for the way God has provided for us financially over the years. I wouldn't say that we are rich today, but our finances are now in order. God is the miracle worker in this story. He has lovingly taken care of every need we have had, and He has also given us the deepest desires of our hearts. He can do it for you, too.

Prayer

Dear Lord, I want to be willing to be willing
for You to take charge of my life. Help me to know
that Your desire is not to harm me but to prosper
me and give me hope and a future [see Jer. 29:11].
Give me the desire to get my finances in order
and become debt free. Amen.

A Path You Never Imagined

*In his heart a man plans his course, but the
LORD determines his steps.*

PROVERBS 16:9

I don't know a single person who enjoys making plans and then having those plans change before they are carried out. Flexibility is a character quality most of us prize, yet it's sometimes difficult to actually feel like being flexible when you're on a different path than you had imagined.

The fact that plans can change is one of life's realities. Sometimes plans change so gradually that we hardly even notice the change as it's happening. Years later we wake up and think, *Whoa, how did things ever get to be like this?* Sometimes plans change radically—in a split second, or overnight. A letter arrives, or we get a phone call, or words are spoken that change everything. Changed plans can involve huge areas of our lives or areas so small they hardly seem consequential. But when we're truthful with ourselves we find that even the small changes in a plan can affect us.

Are you experiencing something right now that you never dreamed would show up on your life's radar screen? What happens when you suddenly find yourself on a path you never imagined? How could you possibly thank God in the middle of such events?

Think with me for a moment about various scenarios.

- Maybe your plan was to graduate from college, work for five years and then have children. But school loans and household expenses have proven larger than you first thought. Graduation was 10 years ago now; you're still in debt, and there are no children in sight.

- Perhaps you and your husband had always counted on his pension when he retired. But last year his company defaulted on its pension plan. Now, instead of retirement being five years away, you're not sure you'll ever be able to scrape enough money together for him to be able to retire.

- Maybe you always assumed that your child would follow Christ when he grew up. You pictured him being an example to his friends, an active participant in your church's youth group and a team member of a summer missions trip when he became a teenager. He's now 16 and wants nothing to do with the Lord.

- Maybe you always planned to grow up and marry your high school sweetheart. Now, due to one mistake you made at a party years ago, you're 33 and a single mother. Your sweetheart has long since married someone else.

- Perhaps you just got word that your father was diagnosed with Alzheimer's. *No way!* you think. *He's way too young for that!*

- Maybe your boss just handed you your pink slip. Lose your job? When was this ever on your life's map? Besides, you're only a couple of months into a new car loan.

What are your changed plans? How hard is it to thank God in the middle of circumstances you never dreamed would happen?

The Plans We Don't See

Plans are not the enemy. Having a plan is vital to living an effective life. Although I'm not a planner by nature, I've learned over the years that plans are important if I'm ever to accomplish all that God desires for my life. I've also learned that a plan can change in a heartbeat.

Have you ever thought for a moment that our plans are not the only plans that exist? When we have faith that God is weaving together all circumstances for the good of those who love Him (see Rom. 8:28), then we get perspective on His plan for our lives. With this perspective, we can have confidence in the words of Proverbs 16:9: "In his heart a man plans his course, but the LORD determines his steps."

You see, our plans are important, but our plans fit into a greater plan—God's plan. Sometimes we see that plan, sometimes we don't. My friend Pat Lewis tells a story of an everyday occurrence that illustrates so well what happens when our plans are revealed in light of God's plans:

The sky opened up and the rain poured down. I rushed to leave my home and get to Carole's house on time for a meeting with the First Place staff and our new pastor. It was very difficult to see in the rainstorm, so I prayed the words of Psalm 139:10, asking the Lord to lead me and hold me by His right hand.

I reached for my cell phone and realized that in my haste to leave, I had left it at home on the charger. I knew it would be foolish to travel without my phone on our busy, construction-laden freeway in this weather, so I hurriedly exited and headed back home. Lost in my thoughts, I traveled several miles before realizing that I was in unfamiliar territory. I felt totally disoriented, and I stopped to ask directions before continuing on.

Now I was late. Frustrated, I asked the Lord why He had allowed me to get lost when I had specifically asked Him to lead me and hold my hand. I thought of the words in

Psalm 34:17: "The righteous cry out, and the LORD hears them; he delivers them from all their troubles." I believed those words and was firmly convinced that the Lord heard my prayer and would lead me and help me arrive safely. I was also delayed in my efforts to reach my destination on time. What could the Lord be doing?

Quickly retrieving my cell phone at the house, I started out again and immediately noticed the rain had subsided; I could now see the roadway better to drive. I began to thank the Lord and continued on my way. After traveling several miles, I suddenly became aware that I had passed three accidents being cleared from the freeway. The Lord quietly spoke to my spirit that if He not led me on a different route than I had planned, I could have been involved in one of the accidents.

81

Immediately, I began to thank Him and praise Him for hearing and answering my prayer, even though my circumstances didn't appear that He had answered. The Lord continued to show me that we cannot trust our circumstances; we can only trust His Word. If we look around us, we have taken our focus and faith off the One who hears and answers prayer and have placed it on what we can see only in the physical realm.

My Plan for Shoes

Problems arise for most of us when all the hard work we've put into planning is seemingly nullified when those plans suddenly change.

How can we get perspective on this?

The answer is not to ignore planning. There are so many things that must be planned before they can be carried out. In my own life, I must plan when I am going to exercise each day. I must plan when I will get up each morning and when I will leave the house. I must plan when I am going to write books, because I work a full-time job and don't have the liberty of writing during my regular work hours. I must plan my travel by purchasing airline tickets and reserving rental vehicles in advance. I must plan for each week in order to lead my First Place class.

At work, our team must plan far into the future for First Place events so that our First Place people can make their plans to attend. We plan our newsletter articles an entire year in advance so that the articles have a common theme each month. Nancy Taylor, our Leadership Training Director, must plan a year in advance for our First Place classes here at Houston's First Baptist Church. Without planning and scheduling, we would not have a room to meet in when it's time for a new session of First Place.

I believe the problem comes when we allow our plans to take precedence over God's plans. An orderly life rarely happens without some planning, yet we must always hold our plans loosely in light of His perfect plan for us.

By learning to be thankful when our plans change, we learn to trust God with our lives. Psalm 37:23-24 says, "The LORD delights in the way of the man whose steps he has made firm; though he stumble, he will not fall, for the LORD upholds him with his hand."

I have learned to laugh and to even enjoy having my plans changed, because I have seen that God's way is always best. When my human plans change, there is a heavenly purpose behind the change.

Let me give you an example. Not long ago, I made a quick trip to Virginia for an appearance on *The 700 Club*. Because I'm not a natural planner, I usually take more clothes and shoes than I need and decide when I get there what I want to wear. For some reason, I wanted this trip to be different. *The 700 Club* asked what color I would wear for the interview, so my clothes were already planned. I got really excited thinking about taking only one outfit and one pair of shoes. I planned to only take one small bag on the trip.

83

The morning I left, I got up at 3:00 A.M. to pack. It was easy to pack my bag with my one outfit and shoes. All I had to do was decide what I was going to wear on the plane. I put on my black loafers, thinking I could wear them on the plane both ways, and left the house feeling really proud of myself.

When I retrieved my loafers from the X-ray machine at the airport, I noticed, to my horror, that I had put on two entirely different shoes! The only similarity was that they were both black. One had a wooden heel and the other had a rubber heel. Usually, I would have had several pairs of shoes to choose from when I arrived at my destination, but this time was different

As I walked away from the security area, I immediately got tickled and began thanking God for this seemingly silly change of plans. I thanked Him that these shoes would serve as a reminder all day that if *The 700 Club* appearance was successful, it was all God's doing, and not mine. I thanked Him that without Him, I am not even capable of choosing two shoes that look alike. I thanked Him that this could be our little joke all day and that this was the worst thing that had happened so far. The entire trip was filled with a sweet awareness that God was going to take care of this scatterbrained woman.

There is tremendous security in resting in God's plans. Sure, we make plans, but if plans change, and they often do, our path is secure in the hands of a loving God.

84

In the Middle of a Changed Plan

When we realize our plans have been changed, it's easy to get frustrated, impatient or even angry that things are not going as expected. But when we realize that we're in the middle of a changed plan, that's the time when God can do a real work in our lives. That's the time to thank Him that He is in control. Even though we may not be able to see the outcome of where He is leading us, we can know from Scripture that His plan for our lives is perfect.

I fully believe what I've just said, even though I can attest to how hard it is at times to get in line with that truth. Not long ago, I spent several hours researching airlines and schedules for some travel I would be doing in the next few weeks. The first trip was to Nashville, and it was a little tricky: On the way back to our home in Texas, I needed to fly from Tennessee directly to California first because Johnny would be there for a doctor's appointment and I wanted to be there with him.

I was extremely pleased when I found a good connecting flight. It would be even better than my first plan. With this flight, I could leave Nashville and fly to Houston first. In Houston, I could connect with Johnny and we could go out to California for the doctor's appointment together. Extra time with my husband is always a bonus.

85

This was a great plan, I thought, and I printed out the itinerary. But something held me back from purchasing the tickets right then and there. Experience has taught me that I should probably call California first and confirm Johnny's appointment. Changing plane tickets once you've bought them is never fun, and we've learned over time to always make sure doctors' appointments are set in stone.

Good thing I called. When I called our doctor's office, I was told that Dr. Bob would be out of town the date of our original appointment and we would need to reschedule for three days afterward. *Hmmmmmm.*

I was so taken aback that I told the receptionist I would need to call her back to reschedule. What was my first response to changed plans? As I hung up the phone, I began to stew and fret about how much work had gone down the tubes. I felt stressed because I would have to go back and figure out different travel plans, and that's never fun. I felt frustration because of the wasted hour I had just spent coming up with this wonderful plan that wouldn't work now. And I felt disappointment because I was really looking forward to having a flight with Johnny.

That was my moment. That was the exact time the Lord chose to do a work in my life. My plans had changed. Could I choose to have faith that He was still in control? Could I be thankful that He had a plan for this trip, even one that I didn't yet see?

Then it hit me. A changed doctor's appointment actually meant that I had been given the gift of time. With the change in plans, I could now return home from Nashville, spend the weekend recuperating at home, wash my clothes, eat a good meal and still leave on Monday with Johnny for California—this time refreshed instead of hurried.

I immediately thanked God that His plan was much better than mine. I thanked Him that I didn't have to lug all my dirty clothes from Nashville to California. I thanked Him for orchestrating my life in such a way that He gives me strength and stamina to continue going forward. I can honestly say that making new airplane reservations didn't take very long at all because I had already done the work of researching schedules. My heart was changed, too. I had quiet confidence again that the Lord was in control—even for something as commonplace as taking a trip.

Safe Footing on God's Solid Ground

It's seldom easy when plans change, because our natural tendency is to cling to what we thought was best. But there is a solution to handling our disgruntlement or dismay over change. The solution is gratitude. Even when we find ourselves on a path we never imagined, we can rest assured that God is in control. God loves us, and He has an amazing and wonderful plan for us. Thanking God when plans change can turn our frustration into acceptance and our stress into peace.

Will you decide to choose this path today?

Prayer

Dear Lord, thank You for changing my plans when they are out of sync with Your plans for my life. Remind me to be thankful when my best-laid plans head south. Help me realize that my plans might not always be best and that Your plans are perfect. Amen.

Peace in a Stressful Season

Cast all your anxiety on him because he cares for you.

1 PETER 5:7

Mmmm, there's nothing like the smell of fresh coffee.

Yesterday, Johnny's brother Mike was here from Austin. They both went down to the pier and I decided to brew up some java for us to enjoy.

Sounded simple enough, right? I made eight cups and poured coffee for the three of us into insulated mugs, placed the mugs on a tray, and started for the back door. When I reached the door, something crazy happened. It was almost like one of those cartoon moments when you see everything in slow motion. Back and forth swayed the mugs on the tray, sort of like when a basketball lollygags around the rim of a basket and you wonder if the shot is actually going to topple in. Well, before I knew it, I had a slam-dunk on my hands! All three mugs toppled over, and three very large cups of fresh-brewed coffee splashed on the dining room floor.

Time out!

My first impulse was to forget the coffee and just clean up the lagoon that had now formed in my dining room and go join Johnny and Mike on the pier. As I took a deep breath, I decided that if it wasn't all that much trouble to make the first eight cups, then making the second eight couldn't be all that hard either. I could mop the floor while the new coffee was brew-ing—now, talk about multi-tasking!

When I look back on this scene now, I realize this moment in my life was a moment of stress. I'm not talking about some sort of huge stress like a loved one dying or needing to declare bankruptcy. This was just one of the everyday, normal stresses that happen a half dozen times a day to all of us. In my case, I had com-pany visiting and I spilled coffee. It wasn't the end of the world, but it was an inconvenience. It slowed me down and had the power to make me feel frustrated if I let it. That's stress.

In this moment, I had a choice to make: I could furrow my brow, hunch my shoulders and mutter angry words under my breath, or I could choose to be thankful.

89

What could I possibly be thankful for in this situa-tion?

Well, how about the fact that I have tile floors, so the coffee wasn't on carpet? *Thanks.*

The sun was out after days of rain and gloom. The temperature was in the mid 70s and there was a mild breeze. *Thanks.*

I was going to be able to rest on the pier on my chaise lounge with a fresh cup of coffee after I finally got the job accomplished. *Thanks.*

Give thanks in all things—even spilled coffee.

I believe there is a simple antidote to the daily stresses and concerns we feel throughout each day. The antidote is—you guessed it: *Begin thanking God for whatever we can in the middle of our stressful situations.* Scripture tells us that God is at work in our lives, even in the midst of something as commonplace as spilled coffee. Small moments can be something He chooses to conform us to the image of His Son.

As you begin to give thanks in all situations, the focus shifts from you and what you are feeling to God and His goodness, and you will begin to feel the stress let up.

That's reason for hope and healing.

The Stress-Solution: Thanksgiving

What are you stressed about right now? Each of us has potential stressors every day, and we can choose how we deal with each one. Our attitude about what is threatening to us is the key to overcoming stress. First Peter 5:7 is a wonderful verse in this area: "Cast all your anxiety on him because he cares for you."

How do we actually "cast" our anxiety on God? Anxiety isn't something touchable like a piece of clothing—it's tough to bundle up anxiety in our hands and throw it into the laundry hamper. No, when God says to cast anxiety upon Him, He asks us to do this through faith, prayer and by understanding His grace. As believers, we can have real confidence that Christ is genuinely concerned about our welfare. Casting our anxiety upon Him is on the same path as recognizing

His love for us. Christ loves us so much that He says in effect, "Don't worry, don't despair—tell me your sorrows and frustrations and let me carry them."

I love how *The Message* paraphrases the words of Christ Jesus in Matthew 11:30:

> Are you tired? Worn out? . . . Come to me. Get away with me and you'll recover your life. I'll show you how to take a real rest. Walk with me and work with me—watch how I do it. Learn the unforced rhythms of grace. I won't lay anything heavy or ill-fitting on you. Keep company with me and you'll learn to live freely and lightly.

91

How wonderful is that! When we give thanks in all situations, we deliberately cast our anxiety on God. Stress can sap our energy and joy. Yet God gives each of us a wonderful antidote for stress, and the antidote is thankfulness. As we start thanking God for whatever we can in the middle of our stressful situation, it's often as if God reaches down and straightens our shoulders, unfurrows our brow and puts a new song in our heart. Often, we can even begin to see a certain amount of humor in our rising frustration and agitation. As we see the humor, we'll begin to laugh about what we are going through, and the stress will begin to melt away.

Choosing to be thankful in the midst of a stressful moment can have an amazing effect. I've seen it time and time again in my own life and in the lives of others. I want to suggest to you three specific ways that being thankful helps overcome stress.

Thankfulness Helps Us Do the Next Right Thing

Have you ever had a season when your to-do list seemed as thick as a phone book? In that season it felt like all the responsibilities and pressures of your life would simply overwhelm you. I've felt the same way too. Sometimes, the stress in those seasons is our own fault—like when we say yes to too many activities, or when our sins and shortcomings create messy situations for us. At other times, stress can simply stack up through no fault of our own like so many dirty dishes in the sink.

In those seasons, I find that giving thanks helps me simply to focus on what I need to do for that one moment. The next moment will come after that, and then after that another moment will come. Step by step, being thankful helps me walk through a full season of life. My task becomes simply to do the next right thing.

I recently had one of those times. My weekend had already been hectic. I drove to San Antonio on a Friday, taught a First Place workshop on Saturday most of the day and drove back home that evening. The next day I taught Sunday School in the morning and had company at the house for the rest of the day. As soon as that company left, I began to get ready for more company who were to stay in our home all week. In the middle of vacuuming the hall carpet, I took stock of the next few days to come: I had a First Place half-time celebration the next day, which entails extra work. The day after that, I had a Bible study in the evening, for which I still had to prepare. The following night my First Place class was going to see the son of one of our members perform in a play.

This was a moment. (You know what I'm talking about.) There, while vacuuming, I realized I could choose to be plenty stressed or I could choose to be thankful. As I reflected through the last few days and my week to come, I began organizing my thoughts, using thankfulness as my guide. I was thankful for a full life—I would rather be a part of purposeful activities any day than sit on my couch watching reruns. I was thankful for company coming—Johnny and I have many dear friends, and we're so glad they are part of our lives. I was thankful to have a house to clean and a vacuum that worked. I was thankful for the simple strength and energy to get up each morning and for a mind that was clear so I could teach and talk and drive and function. It's always a temptation to take health for granted.

93

Sure, I could get plenty stressed, but I chose not to. When I chose thankfulness, I could concentrate on doing the next right thing. One activity would follow the next. To get through that season, I simply needed to take one step at a time.

Thankfulness Gives Us New Perspective

Think back to a recent time when you have been stressed. It might be that you were stuck in traffic for over an hour because of a wreck ahead of you. Let's add some rain to that scenario. Thank God that you have a car and weren't sitting on a bicycle in the rain. Thank God that you have air conditioning (or heat) and you weren't sitting in the sweltering heat or freezing cold. Thank God that your life was spared and that you were not in the wreck; and pray for the people who were (and their caregivers).

Maybe you're stressed right now because of a lack of money in your life. Yesterday, I called one of my First Place members on my drive home. She has been going through a season of financial hardship. She had missed our meeting and I wanted to check on her. She told me about going to the bank to deposit $100 into her account. When her receipt was printed out, the balance showing on the receipt was way too much. As she stood there thinking this couldn't possibly be her bank balance, she realized that the overage was a direct deposit of her income tax refund check to her account. She stood there thanking and praising God for His provision.

Maybe the state of your marriage has you in great distress. Why not try thanking God for anything remotely good about your spouse? Start a list in your journal. Every time you think of something positive, write it down. After a few days of doing this, try telling your spouse some of the things you have written in your journal. As you begin exercising these positive steps, your stress level will ease and you will be able to see the situation with more clarity.

When we give thanks in the midst of whatever stressful situation we're in, we can gain a whole new perspective on things. A friend of mine who grew up in a small town in northwest Ohio illustrates this point so well.

She attended one school system her whole life, always went to the same church and married her high school sweetheart. She and her husband bought a house across the road from his parents, just three miles away from the home where her parents lived. Children came along, and as they grew they became friends with children of friends that the woman and her husband had grown up with.

My friend loved her life and the closeness and stability she felt from deeply planted roots. All that changed one day when her husband got a job transfer to Florida. How could the family ever leave everything they had ever known—parents, friends, church, schools, hometown? Some people were even angry with them for taking the transfer.

My friend wrote:

> At first, I felt like I was planning a funeral with no physical body. Inside I was grieving for the loss of the familiar, the history, the relationships my children would have with all their grandparents and friends. One day I remembered advice that I had once given to someone else moving across country—God is already there. I began to

feel some peace knowing that God had a plan for us. He already had people lined up waiting to bless us when we got to our new home, and I was sure that He would use us to bless them also. I had an attitude change and sincerely began to support my husband in the choice he was making for our family and his career.

I realized so much of this move was going to be about perspective. My attitude could make or break how those close to us responded to the move and how our children would react to the change.

As I began to give thanks in the midst of this situation, I had to ask myself: *Really, what was the big deal about moving compared to what so many other families go through?* Our children were healthy. My husband had a good job. We weren't counting on my job for financial support. Some of my husband's coworkers had been transferred out of the country. We were only going to be 4 hours away by plane or 21 hours away by car. I began to give thanks for what we *did* have and not focus on what we were losing.

Many other families have moved and survived, and we could too.

That's the perspective that being thankful can bring. My friend said later that the move turned out quite well in the end. The family established new friendships that soon became dear to them. They were blessed to be able to travel frequently to see their parents, and those visits became extra special. Everyone in their new neighborhood had been transplanted from somewhere else—everyone was without roots in this new community—and the family was used by the Lord to minister to and show compassion to other families in the area.

Thankfulness Allows Us to Focus on the Positive

I believe our God is able to work absolute wonders on our behalf if we can learn to thank and praise Him in the middle of any stressful situation of life. When we're not thankful, we tend to focus on what's wrong. When we focus on the muck and grime of stressful situations, we begin to grumble and complain—and that makes the situation appear worse than it actually is. Think about it. Have you ever noticed that stress is intensified when we speak negative words?

97

Making statements such as the following are sure-fire stress intensifiers:

- I hate my job.
- My kids are driving me crazy.
- My life is impossible.
- No one cares about me.

You might be going through a difficult time—and it's good to know the truth of any situation. For example, you may actually have a difficult or ill-fitting job; your kids may be misbehaving; your life may have a number of painful realities, or it may seem like your friends and family members disregard your feelings. Yet in the midst of a stressful situation, you still have a choice whether or not to compound the problem. Speaking negative words will do that.

The Bible gives us the kind of words to speak that will ease our stress. Philippians 4:8 says, "Finally, brothers, whatever is true, whatever is noble, whatever is right, whatever is pure, whatever is lovely, whatever is admirable—if anything is excellent or praiseworthy—think about such things."

How can you realize the truth of a situation and still praise God in the midst of it? With a thankful attitude, you may find yourself praying to the Lord, with words such as:

- God, my job is not ideal, yet thank You that I have a job, and thank You that this job won't last forever. Thank You that I'm learning things here that I know I couldn't learn anywhere else.
- Lord, my kids are driving me nuts, yet thank You so much for my children. Thank You that You gave them to me with all their strengths and weaknesses and that You believe I am capable of helping to nurture and guide these little lives as they grow up.

- Father, I can name five things right now that just seem impossible—I don't know how things will ever be worked out. But right now I thank You because You *do* know how things will be resolved. You are in control and You are good, and I thank You for who You are.
- Jesus, it seems like no one cares for me right now, but I want to thank You because I know You care for me. Friends and family members will let me down, but You will never leave me nor forsake me. Thank You.

Can't you just feel the tension being lifted when you speak such positive words about a negative situation? Conversely, the negative things we think about long enough will invariably work their way out of our mouths. After we have thought negatively for a while and then speak negatively about our situation or about a person, the stress begins to intensify.

The solution is found in Philippians 4:8. We must steep our lives in thanksgiving and choose to always see the hand of a good God in our lives.

The Unforced Rhythms of Grace

God's intention is never for us to stuff our stress deep down in our souls where it festers and rips away at our insides. His intention is for us to give our stress to Him. The Bible tells us the truth about our life, and this truth has the power to replace all the lies we tell ourselves when we are stressed. Our attitude about a situation is the key to relieving our stress. Remember, attitudes follow actions, not the other way around. You can take the action of being thankful today.

One of my favorite verses has become Romans 15:13: "May the God of hope fill you with all joy and peace as you trust in him, so that you may overflow with hope by the power of the Holy Spirit." What a stress-relieving verse for our lives!

Prayer

Dear Father, I am really tired and weary because of the stressful life I live. Help me remember to start thanking You for whatever I can the next time I start feeling stressed. I ask You to work in my heart in this area until I can honestly say that I am no longer living a stress-filled life. Amen.

What Every Family Needs

If anyone does not provide for his relatives, and especially for his immediate family, he has denied the faith.

I TIMOTHY 5:8

Family.

Has there ever been a word that can evoke as much emotion as this word?

What feelings do you get when you think about your family—both the family you grew up in and the family you have now? Take a moment to think about your parents, brothers, sisters, children and grandchildren (if you have them), grandparents, uncles, aunts, cousins and in-laws.

Is there joy and excitement when you think of each person? Do you feel a tender surge of nostalgia? A flash of wonderful years spent in security and happiness? Or is there sadness, anxiety, maybe even anger or rage? Do you look upon family members with regret and disappointment? Do they feel like a weight on your shoulders or a dark splotch in your thoughts?

Maybe, like most people, your family is somewhere in between. Sure, your family is great, but there are some problems. Family gatherings carry a mixture of happiness and discomfort or even sadness. It's great to be with everyone, but there are pockets of hurt, as well.

What is your family like?

Cindy's Story

My friend Cindy was struggling with family. Her 18-year-old son, Joey, had decided he could no longer live by the family rules. Cindy and her husband made the toughest decision they had ever made when, after repeated failed attempts to get their son back on track, they asked him to leave their home.

Cindy said it felt like her heart had been yanked out of her chest. Her son left, and she had no idea where he had gone. She knew she needed God ever so close to her. As she continued to bathe the situation in prayer, she kept hearing the phase: "Thank God for everything. Even this."

It was not easy to pray, yet Cindy began to thank the Lord for everything she could think of that related to the path her son was choosing.

Over the next few months, a quiet transformation began to take place in the most unusual ways.

Joey found places to stay with various friends. A few were from Christian homes; a few were not. At one point, he stayed with one friend whose mother was what Joey called a "biker mom." She rode a Harley, had multiple tattoos and spiky hair and her house was always a party hangout where teenagers could drink and get free condoms.

In spite of differences in their homes, the biker mom made Joey contact Cindy once a week to let Cindy know how he was doing. The biker mom also phoned Cindy often to talk about Joey and the situation. Cindy said she soon learned that God's gifts come in strange packages and to be grateful for them and not to judge.

Joey had always dreamed of being in the Air Force, but he had gained too much weight in high school to enlist. In the time he spent with the biker mom, Joey had to walk anywhere he needed to go. Walking helped him lose the weight he needed in order to enlist. He also had no money and needed to pass summer school to get into the service, so he found a job mowing lawns to pay for his classes. When Joey lived at home, he had always struggled with getting out of bed. But with nobody around to tell him what to do, he found he needed to take the initiative himself.

103

Today, Joey is thriving in the Air Force. The independence and confidence he learned as a result of the tough decision his parents made gave him the necessary tools to learn true responsibility. His relationship with his parents is back on track, and he has an ongoing relationship with his biker mom.

Cindy says that when she began thanking God in the midst of a situation that seemed unbearable, God revealed His love, grace and provision in ways she never could have imagined.

What Every Family Needs

It's not always easy to thank the Lord in the midst of difficult family situations. Emotions are so powerful when it comes to the people closest to us. Often, our feelings toward our families are colored by negative character traits we see in ourselves, which further compounds the issue. For example, Grandma may have always been a critical person, so Mama was a critical person, too, and now you struggle with being critical. Or, Grandpa was an angry person, so Daddy was always angry. Now, anger is a trait that characterizes your life.

What's the solution here? When we look at our families, patterns often repeat themselves. We do the same thing, over and over, while hoping for a different result. If we didn't receive something we deemed was important, we go through life trying to get someone to give it to us.

It's up to us to help break the pattern.

If it isn't difficult for you to always be thankful for your family, that's wonderful. But chances are there are moments when "thankful" is not one of the words that comes to mind when you think of family. I hope this chapter will help us all see how thankfulness can bring healing not only to us but to our families as well.

I want to suggest something you might consider quite radical in your efforts to be a pattern-breaker. Chances are, you didn't receive something you needed from certain family members, and you've wasted a lot of time trying to receive that particular something from those people (who may not have a clue about your need).

I strongly believe that we can break that pattern by reversing the trend. We can get what we've missed, not by grasping or clutching from those people, but by giving to them.

What a plan! Simply *start giving to your family members*. I'm talking about the type of lavish giving that expects nothing in return. For example, if we give to our parents the respect, courtesy and gentleness that we needed from them but perhaps didn't receive, I believe that God will begin a healing work between our parents and us. If we begin giving our spouses the admiration, encouragement and unconditional love they perhaps didn't receive from their parents, God will begin healing our marriage. If we, as parents, begin giving our children the love, attention, boundaries and devotion we perhaps never received during our growing-up years, God will begin healing our children.

105

There are two verses I find extremely helpful here: First, our God is a master at restoring the years the locusts have eaten (see Joel 2:25), and second, "He has made everything beautiful in its time" (Eccles. 3:11). Your family may be ravaged by years of emotional, spiritual and physical hardship. Yet God can heal your family. He can make it beautiful, in His time, in His way, perhaps in ways you never imagined, but beautiful nonetheless. Our God can work miracles in the people closest to you.

What is our part in this?

I believe there are four basic things we all need. When we don't receive one or more of these things, there is a gaping hole in our heart. That hole often causes us to do really strange things when it comes to our family. Sometimes we continue trying to get whatever it is we are missing from a parent or grandparent. Or, even worse, since we didn't get it growing up, we might try to get it from our spouse or, yes, even our children.

What are the four things that every human being needs? *Attention, affirmation, appreciation* and *affection*. God has hardwired us so that we are full of holes without these things. Let's look at each one and ask God to show us ways that we can begin giving these to our families.

Attention

Johnny and I have two cats, a dog and a bird that absolutely demand our attention. The cats bump our hands with their heads until we pet them; the dog paws us until we pet his head or rub his back; the bird screeches until we walk over to his cage and take him out. If animals, who have no soul, need this type of attention, then what does attention (or the lack of) mean to human beings, who are created in the image of God?

When we give another person true attention, we are acknowledging that he or she has needs and we are taking the time to meet those needs. A baby has a lot of needs; but as a baby grows and becomes more independent, his or her demands are not as great. Most of us had our basic needs met as a baby. We were fed, bathed, dressed and taught the basic needs to survive.

But this type of basic, need-meeting attention is not what I'm talking about here. All of us give this sort of attention to our families every day. Caring for the physical needs of our family is very different from the true attention we all need.

I call this type of attention noticing someone with a capital N. It means we truly see the people in our lives and we see them through Christ's eyes—with compassion, importance, value and love.

Some of us slip into the very pattern with our children that we hated to see in our parents while we were growing up; we stay so busy that we hardly notice that others around us have needs. We fill our lives with jobs, friends, hobbies, service organizations or church work so that there is no time left to notice the only ones who might really care if we were no longer around.

107

My husband was reared by good parents. His dad worked every day and paid all the bills. His mom stayed home and cooked, washed and ironed the clothes and cleaned the house. In many ways, this would seem like an ideal environment to grow up in, but there was something lacking that is so vital to a child.

Johnny's dad gave the boys a bit of attention because he coached Johnny and his older brother in baseball. Other than that, he pretty much stayed behind the newspaper when he was home and worked the rest of the time. Although he was a moral, ethical man, he never took his family to church. Ten years after Weldon and Johnny were born, two more boys were born into the family. They received even less attention, because Daddy was older and didn't have the energy to coach the two younger boys.

Their mom, on the other hand, showed attention to them the only way she knew how: through acts of service. You see, her own mom had died when she was five years old, and she and her sister became the caregivers for the entire family. As children, they cooked, cleaned and did the laundry for their dad and four brothers. Johnny knew in his heart that his mom loved him, but it still hurts him to this day that he can't remember her ever holding him on her lap when he was a child or telling him that she loved him.

108

Giving attention to others takes time. So if we didn't receive the attention we needed as children, it is really easy as adults to stay so busy that it appears to others we do not have the time for them. When we pay attention to our family, we are showing that we are thankful they're in our lives. Paying attention includes things like listening when they talk or taking the time to play a game or just visit for a while. It means never acting like we're too busy to be with them, even if it just means listening while they talk.

In what ways can you truly show attention to your family members today?

Affirmation

Every human being has some good qualities, talents and abilities. You might be thinking, *Not my dad; not my husband; not my daughter.* This kind of thinking comes from not receiving the affirmation you needed as a child. If your parents never recognized the good things about you, it will be harder for you to recognize the good things about others.

Negative parents have a way of raising negative children. I have friends that have no idea how negative they are. Every conversation takes a negative bent, and their own personal cup is always half-empty instead of half-full. I am by nature a very positive person; but something weird happens when I spend a lot of time with negative people. Instead of me pulling them up, they tend to drag me down. Therefore, it is easy to see how being raised by one or two parents who were negative, perfectionistic, demanding or critical will make it harder to give to others those things that we lack.

109

How do we affirm someone in our family? Simply, by stating something positive about them. What does your family member do well? Is your mom a fabulous cook? Is your dad great at fixing things? Does your spouse keep a clean house or pay the bills on time? Do your children have athletic or musical talent?

Tell them! Affirm them by writing them a note. Send an e-mail. Phone if they live far away. Sometimes it's hard to say something directly, but somehow, some way, find a way to communicate your affirmation of them.

Remember, whatever you say must be true. If it isn't true, your family member will see right through it and the healing that you so desperately desire will not happen.

By affirming our family members, we are telling them we're thankful for them. As we affirm them, God will start the healing in our lives as well.

What ways can you affirm your family members today?

Appreciation

When we begin affirming our family members, a funny thing happens. Before long, we start appreciating them. While affirmation is simply saying something positive that is true, appreciation taps into our feelings about the positive things we say. By showing apprecia-tion, we're learning how to be truly thankful for our family members.

110

Yesterday, when I got home from work, I thought a professional cleaning service had somehow unlocked our front door and done a number on our house while I was gone. Everything looked different. Things were tidied and stacked. The dishwasher was running. Even our two refrigerators were clean. As I stood with my mouth open, looking at the cleaning miracle, Johnny proudly explained that he had done the job.

In the span of 46 years of marriage, this has never happened before. My husband is simply not the house-cleaning type. And refrigerators? That really took the cake!

Can you imagine how he might have felt if I had said something like, "Well it's about time" or "Now you know how hard it has been for me to clean the refrigerator all these years"?

Instead, I spent the evening telling him how much I appreciated all his hard work. I didn't tell him just once. First, I said, "They are so clean! You did it better than me!" After dinner, I said I couldn't believe that on such a beautiful day he had worked so hard inside the house. After assuring me that once he got started he just couldn't quit, I told him again how much we were going to enjoy those clean refrigerators this weekend. Before we went to sleep, I told him how much I loved him and how he still surprises me after all these years.

You see, affirmation would have been stating the truth: "You did a good job of cleaning the refrigerator." But appreciation is putting some feeling into the affirmation. Appreciation will work miracles with just about anyone. After you have practiced affirmation by stating positive truths to your family members, take it a little further. Start putting some emotion and feeling into those positive statements with appreciation—say words such as, "I love it when you do that" and "I'm so proud of you."

Not everyone will have someone clean their house for them, but what ways can you find to applaud and appreciate your family members today?

Affection

Last, but not least, is the role that affection plays in the life of our family members. I'm talking about a specific type of affection that can bring up a number of emotions depending on our backgrounds. I'm talking about physical affection—touch. Physical affection is so important, because we absolutely can't do without it. Physical affection will help bring total healing to fractured hearts.

A dear friend of mine decided that she was going to start showing affection to her father. She adores her dad but he had never been good at showing physical affection to her, which in turn, has caused her problems. It's been hard for her to show physical affection to her husband and her own daughter. She shared with me what motivated her to become the initiator of change.

112

She and her dad had both come separately to a church convention. My friend worked a booth, while her dad mingled on the floor where he had run into the family's former pastor. As my friend's dad and the pastor walked up to her, the pastor gave my friend a big bear hug, and my friend's dad stuck out his hand. A hug and a handshake—it didn't get any more obvious than that.

My friend said that learning to give affection didn't happen overnight. But little by little, as she started giving her dad hugs, her dad learned not only to receive her hugs but to return them as well. By the time her dad died and went on to heaven, the hole in my friend's heart had been healed. She believes the hole in her dad's heart was healed as well.

Affection will look different in different families, depending on how close people are and how comfortable they are with affection. Here are some ways you might give affection to your family:

- Give your son a pat on the back for a job well done.
- Kiss your mom and dad on the cheek when coming over to their house.
- Ask everybody to hold hands around the dinner table while giving thanks for the food and the time together.
- Sit with your arm around your elderly mom in the nursing home.
- Give your adult brother a warm handshake whenever you meet.
- Give your grandchildren hugs when you leave their house.

113

When it comes to affection, be mindful of people's comfort level, but be proactive, too. Take the initiative when it comes to telling people that you care for them and are thankful for them. You'll be so thankful you did, and so will the ones you love.

Thankful for Family

There are so many types of families today. People have helpful and harmful families, and everything in between. Regardless of the family you originally came from and the family you have today, the Lord is calling you to be thankful for your family members.

You may not feel thankful for everyone in your family, but you can be proactive in that process. Thankfulness can be expressed by attention, affirmation, appreciation and affection.

Start practicing these four traits with the people closest to you and watch the hope and healing begin.

Prayer

*Dear Lord, I love my family, but sometimes
I have a really hard time showing it. I ask You
to help me give attention, affirmation, appreciation
and affection to all the members of my family.
Heal every hurt in our hearts and make
us truly thankful that we are related
to each other. Amen.*

When Rock Bottom Draws You Near

You're blessed when you're at the end of your rope.
MATTHEW 5:3, *THE MESSAGE*

I have a dear friend, Elizabeth Crews, who works as an addictions counselor and is also one of our First Place Networking Leaders in California. Since Elizabeth works in the area of addictions every day, I asked her to share her story about her own food addiction for this chapter.

Elizabeth's story is no different from yours or mine if we struggle with any kind of addiction. The specific substance or activity—whether it is food, drugs, alcohol, gambling, shopping, pornography or sex—is not the problem. The problem comes when we depend on any substance or activity because it soothes us or numbs our pain.

If you know or suspect that you have an addiction, the only way you will ever find permanent healing is to allow God to heal you. Alcoholics Anonymous groups refer to God as a "higher power" because many alcoholics don't believe in or pray to God for deliverance from their addiction. As Christians, our higher power is God, His Son, Jesus Christ, and the Holy Spirit. All three will come into our lives if we will cry out to them for the help and healing we so desperately need.

Here is Elizabeth's story.

An Upbringing of Need

Like many of you, the family I grew up in was defined by scarcity. Survival mode was the order of the day. Not only were my ancestors from frugal Scottish stock but also my parents had lived through the poverty of the Great Depression. Even though America was in the post-World War II boom when I grew up, in my mother's mind there would never be enough. As a result, I grew up in poverty and deprivation.

In retrospect, I can see that we weren't really poor; we were a middle-class family. My father was in the military. We had a steady income source and my parents owned a home. They even had a modest savings account. But as I learned at a very early age, poverty is not just an economic reality but it is also a state of mind. My mother compulsively hoarded and saved in anticipation of the rainy day she was convinced loomed just around the corner. The word "abundance" was not part of our family vocabulary. Instead, I grew up in a home characterized by "never enough."

Perhaps that is why I was so taken aback when the presenter at a vocational discernment seminar I once attended asked the question "What do you have an abundance of?" My first reaction was, "Abundance? I don't have an abundance of anything. Life is about scarcity and struggle and eking out a living in a land filled with briars and thorns." As the presenter persisted with his question "What do you have an abundance of?" the next thought that popped into my head was "words."

Anyone who knows me would agree with that conclusion! I am seldom at a loss for words—and I am known for adding my two cents to any discussion, whether or not it is asked for, let alone wanted. Beyond the verbosity, there was more. Packed away in boxes and file drawers I had a virtual treasure trove of written-down words. Some were contained in prayer journals I had kept for years. Others were the verses, poems, quotes and teaching stories I had collected. There were notes I had taken at seminars, promising myself I would study them at a later date. There were file folders marked "for review" and scraps of paper with notes and thoughts scribbled across them. There was also the treasure chest of words stored inside my heart. Memorizing Scripture was something I had consistently done for years.

117

At that seminar, I discovered that I was living in self-imposed scarcity, even though God had promised abundance to those He loves. I realized that I had an abundance of raw material packed away, waiting to be woven into writings designed to give understanding, encouragement and hope to God's people. I left the seminar that day with a dream and a clear sense of my vocation and calling. But there was one obstacle I would need to overcome before my newfound vision could become reality.

My Addiction

There was another item I could have put on my "what I have an abundance of" list that day: excess body weight. Although my family of origin did without many things, there was always an abundance of food in the house. Cabinets packed with food were part of my mother's hoarding and represented her fear of not having enough. As long as we had food, we would be okay, and food was the cure for all ills. At an early age, I learned to turn to food for comfort, solace, companionship and love. As a result of growing up in a less-than-nurturing family, there was a hole in my soul so large that I could hear the wind whistling through it on a stormy day! I compulsively tried to fill this inner emptiness with outer substances—especially with food.

118

Although I could exercise self-discipline in some areas of my life, I could not control my eating. Not only did my disordered relationship with food have progressive health consequences but also my out-of-control eating kept me from realizing my God-given calling and vocation. Each time I stood before a class to teach or sat down to write an article on living a disciplined Christian life, I came face-to-face with my lack of discipline in the area of food. I once heard a speaker at an Overeaters' Anonymous meeting say, "A compulsive overeater is never anonymous." Those words were certainly true of my life. No matter how eloquent my words, my body contradicted my profession that Christ was the Lord of my life.

It became increasingly clear to me that if I was going to realize my dream of illuminating God's Word in a way that gave understanding and led to changed lives, I would need to first confront my own disobedience that kept me in defeat and separated me from God's blessings. In the words of Jeremiah 5:25, "[my] sins [had] deprived [me] of good."

God's Plan or Mine?

In *The Message*, Eugene Peterson paraphrases Matthew 5:3 (Jesus' first beatitude) this way: "You're blessed when you're at the end of your rope. With less of you there is more of God and his rule."

119

Those words certainly described the state of my life when I finally came to the understanding that if I was going to realize God's plans for my life, I was going to have to get my eating under control. Of course, I had been on and off diets all of my adult life; diets that promised quick results but in reality were part of the problem, not part of the solution.

Sure, I could lose weight; but deprivation only set me up to binge and regain all the weight I had lost, plus more. It became a vicious yo-yo cycle, and each failure further eroded my self-esteem and confidence. Another diet was definitely not the answer. I was at the end of my rope, but I didn't realize that the root of my problem was not about food at all—the only lasting solution would be to allow God to fill that inner longing that no amount of food in the world could satisfy.

Adding to the irony of the situation was the fact that I am a trained addictions counselor. For more than 15 years, I helped others overcome the cycle of addiction and repeated relapse, yet I was totally power-less to help myself. After all, "they" were addicts who had hit bottom and had no choice but to surrender their lives to God. I just had a problem with food, a problem I could overcome anytime I set my mind to do so. Oh, certainly I joked about being a chocoholic with an addiction to sugar, but I didn't take my disorder-ed relationship with food seriously or treat it like an addiction.

120

I was not willing to set a bottom-line behavior regarding my eating and to not cross that boundary, no matter what. Somehow I failed to equate a candy bar that was not on my food plan with a drink that sent the alcoholic back to the addiction cycle. Neither was I willing to give up the people, places and things that were part of my out-of-control eating. As a result of my denial about the true cause of my overeating—a cunning, baffling and powerful addiction to certain foods—I sank deeper and deeper into the progressive nature of addiction where enough is never enough.

Where Wisdom Begins

There is an old Chinese epigram that states that the beginning of wisdom is to call things by their right name. Until I was willing to call my relationship with food by its right name—addiction—I was powerless to arrest the disease that permeated every fiber of my being.

Addiction, at its core, is the continued use of any process or substance in spite of adverse consequences. And whether or not I liked the word "addiction," I had to admit that my chronic out-of-control eating had resulted in some very adverse consequences that had progressed over time and were now impacting every aspect of my being. Although I had been a Bible-believing Christian for many years, I had not surrendered my life to God's will and His Word when it came to caring for my body as His holy temple.

121

When I was at the end of my rope, God also brought me to the First Place program. Through a set of circumstances that only He could have orchestrated, I was introduced to a weight-loss program with biblical integrity that was able to address my true need—a relationship with the true and living God. As I put the nine commitments that First Place espouses into practice, Matthew's words about "less of me making more room for God" took on a new meaning.

When Carole Lewis first talked to me about writing a piece on thankfulness, I quickly went into my professional self and wrote a piece on addiction as a means of grace. It was heady and factual and presented a textbook approach to the correlation between gratitude and quality recovery. But Carole didn't want my professional writing; she wanted the story that had come from my own personal struggle with addiction. *Easy,* I thought. But as one day followed another, and writing my personal thankfulness-in-addiction testimony somehow never made it to the top of my to-do list, I began to suspect there was a reason behind my procrastination that went beyond the excuses I was giving myself. Writer's block is something I had never before experienced, and now I found myself staring at a blank computer screen, wondering why the words did not flow onto the page.

Not knowing what else to do, I began to pray. Certainly, I was thankful for having found the First Place program. I was thankful that by following the nine commitments of First Place my life had been visibly transformed. Now I could stand before a room full of people without the negative voices convincing me that I was a hypocrite because my body belied my words. I was realizing my dream of writing, and I was thankful that God was opening doors that allowed me to use my spiritual gifts for His glory. My quiet time had become the mainstay of my life and I could feel God's love and presence surrounding me no matter what else was happening around me.

As I began to pray, I realized I had so much to be thankful for. My health was being renewed and my relationship with God was vibrant and interactive. Why couldn't I write about being thankful for my addiction? After all, had it not been for the addiction, none of these benefits would have come into my life. And then I recalled the key verse Carole had chosen for her book on thankfulness: "Give thanks in all circumstances" (1 Thess. 5:18). God was not asking me to be thankful for my addictive relationship with food. This cunning, baffling and powerful addiction had been the root cause of pain and sorrow—and it was never God's will that I replace my need for Him with a love-hate relationship with food! Nowhere in God's Word are we told to give thanks for evil!

What His Word told me was to give thanks in spite of my addictive relationship with food. I was to give thanks during the adverse trials He sent into my life to perfect my faith. I was being asked to give thanks that this powerful addiction had finally brought me to my knees—to the end of my rope—so there would be room for God and His Lordship in my life. I was to give thanks because in the midst of my pain and sorrow God sent forth His Word and healed me. When all seemed lost, He brought me to the First Place program where I found peace and harmony and balance—and a right relationship with God.

When I began to meditate on how God had redeemed my life from the pit of the addictive cycle, I began to overflow with thankfulness. He had indeed set me free from the prison of an addictive relationship with food so that I could worship Him in spirit and in truth. That alone was reason for profound gratitude. With the apostle Paul, I could rejoice always, not because my circumstances were joyful but because the Lord was near. God would never leave me to face my problems alone, and He had promised to lead me to victory if I would just be still and let Him be the Lord of my life. God's love, not my adversity, was the reason I could give thanks in all circumstances. And that fact alone is reason for thanksgiving!

When Rock Bottom Draws You Near

Every night before I drift off to sleep, I say the words to Psalm 103:1-5. It's the same psalm that Carole wrote about in depth in chapter 4. My prayer is that you too can find reason to praise God in these words written centuries ago by David.

> Praise the LORD, O my soul;
> all my inmost being, praise his holy name.
> Praise the LORD, O my soul,
> and forget not all his benefits—
> who forgives all your sins
> and heals all your diseases;
> who redeems your life from the pit
> and crowns you with love and compassion.
> who satisfies your desires with good things
> so that your youth is renewed like the eagle's.
> Praise the LORD, O my soul.
> (Psalm 103:1-5,22)

Those of us who have been freed from the pit of addiction know what it is like to praise the Lord for all

His benefits. We know firsthand what it's like to have our diseases healed, our sins forgiven, our life redeemed and our desires satisfied with good things.

The Son has set us free, and we are free indeed.

Prayer

Dear Lord, You know me inside and out. You know all the reasons I became addicted and all the excuses I use for staying addicted to _____.
I ask You to heal me, from the inside-out, of this addiction to _____. After I am healed, I pray You will use me to help others break free from their addictions. Amen.

125

Thriving with an Ever-Present Problem

[Nothing] will be able to separate us from the love of God.

ROMANS 8:39

Chronic illness is something my husband, Johnny, and I struggle with, even as I write this book. It is a constant part of our lives, yet the Lord has enabled us to give thanks in the midst of everything—even today.

My sweet husband likes to say that he always knew there were two things he would not die from: cancer or a heart attack. Johnny always believed that if you ate a healthy diet and were active, these two conditions could be prevented. We have learned that life has a way of not playing out as we planned. I would never have believed that we could be thankful while living with cancer, but God has shown us how to do it.

A Journey into Hurt

In October 1997, Johnny felt a faint pain in his groin area. He had undergone surgery for a hernia in this same area about 12 years before, so he assumed that the hernia was back. He decided to bypass our family doctor and asked me to make an appointment with the surgeon who had performed the hernia surgery. After examining Johnny, the surgeon said, "It's not a hernia. You need to see a urologist."

After examining Johnny, the urologist took six biopsies of Johnny's prostate, drew blood and sent him home to wait for the results. The next week was our First Place F.O.C.U.S. Week, so we were in Round Top, Texas, the entire week. Johnny and our daughters, Lisa and Shari, were cooking for the event, so we were all busy enough that we hardly thought about the test results. We returned home on Thursday to find out that our son's home had burned to the ground that day.

It's an amazing story, and it digresses from the subject of chronic illness, but you will begin to understand why we didn't have time to worry, much less think about, Johnny's test results. Plus, it's another illustration of how you can give thanks in all circumstances, whether you receive a bad health diagnosis or your home burns to the ground.

127

Lisa, John's wife, (my daughter and my daughter-in-law are both named Lisa) mowed the yard that morning and parked the riding mower in the garage near the hot water heater. She went inside, showered and dressed herself and Harper, their little girl, and left to take Harper to a Mother's Day Out event at their church. She and John planned to meet back at the house for lunch.

John arrived home before Lisa. He drove up and watched as the firemen battled the fire consuming their home. A few minutes later, Lisa arrived, and together they watched their home burn to the ground. That evening, all five of them arrived at our home with only the clothes they were wearing that day. Everything else was gone.

What could we be thankful for in this situation? Well, there were many things.

- We were thankful that Lisa and Harper were alive. They had only been gone a few minutes when the hot water heater exploded into flames. The garage was attached to the kitchen, so if Lisa and Harper had been in the kitchen, they would have surely been killed.
- We were thankful that they only lived one mile from our home, so the children could still ride the same bus and have as little disruption as possible in their daily routines.
- We were thankful that much of what they needed, such as sheets, towels, toothpaste, soap, washer and dryer, was already available in our home.
- We were thankful for friends who immediately rallied around to help. John's office requested the three children's clothes sizes and that very evening brought two outfits with underwear and shoes for each of the children. My office brought over everything they could think of to help. My Sunday School class took up an offering for imme-

diate needs that John and his family might have.

· We were thankful that John and Lisa were able to leave the children with us that night and go to the store to buy diapers for Harper and all the various other things they needed.

Think about losing everything you own in the space of 30 minutes—whether it's your house or your health. Would you, could you, be thankful in that situation? One of the things John and Lisa were most thankful for was that just prior to the fire, Lisa had taken every one of their family pictures and put them in a trunk, planning to put together some albums at a later date. She slid the trunk under their bed. It was one of the few things that survived with very little damage. Isn't God good?

129

As I said, with all that was going on in our lives, you can understand why we didn't have time to worry, much less think about, Johnny's test results.

The Monday after the fire, I dropped Johnny off at the hospital for a day of tests. He was scheduled for a CT scan and bone scan. During lunch, I was interviewing a lady for a job and planned to meet Johnny at the hospital afterward. As we were having lunch, the lady I was interviewing shared that her husband had died of cancer. Innocently, I inquired about the type of cancer.

"Prostate cancer," she said.

"How long did he live with the cancer?" I asked

"Eight months."

I left our lunch meeting and drove to the hospital with a heavy dread hovering around me. While I sat in the waiting room waiting for Johnny to finish his bone scan, the doctor in charge of nuclear medicine at the hospital walked into the waiting room. I immediately recognized him as our former internist. He stopped to say hello and asked me who I was waiting for. When I told him it was my husband, he said some words that changed our family's life.

"Honey, you need to come into my office for a minute," he said.

When a doctor takes you aside like that, it can only be for one reason.

Living with a Bad Diagnosis

After I was seated, the doctor filled me in on the morning's events. Johnny was having his second bone scan to confirm that the first one was accurate, but the diagnosis was fairly certain: prostate cancer that had already spread to Johnny's bones. They found spots on his pelvic bone, which was where the pain in the groin was coming from.

What do you do when you receive shattering news? I had already collapsed in tears when Johnny came walking into the office to hear the news himself. Johnny was his usual calm self, sitting there listening as the doctor shared again everything he had told me. The doctor also shared that he had spoken with our urologist and that five out of six of Johnny's biopsy sites were malignant. He told us how sorry he was as we stood up, thanked him and walked out of the hospital.

By this time, I was sobbing and was a complete mess. Johnny hadn't eaten all day because of the tests and was starving. Not knowing what kind of news we might receive, we had told the kids that we were going to drive to the Bay and spend the night there. As we drove toward the Bay, Johnny wanted to eat at one of his favorite Mexican restaurants on that side of town. By the time he parked in front of the restaurant, I was in the worst shape possible. It was October and already dark outside, but Johnny suggested that I put on his sunglasses so that no one would see how swollen my eyes were. We proceeded inside and took a table in the corner with me facing the wall. It was a surreal feeling to be able to laugh through my tears about how all the customers and wait staff must think that the reason I had on sunglasses and was crying was because my husband was a wife beater! We also were able to laugh about the fact that even though I was an emotional basket case, I was able to eat all of my dinner!

131

After dinner we drove to our little Bay house where I proceeded to cry for the next three days. Johnny was the one with the cancer, but he was calm and tried to console me. After three days, I looked at him and said, "I'm just so sorry that I can't be strong for you right now." Johnny replied, "How do you think I would feel if you were strong right now? It comforts me to know how much you care."

The next couple of weeks were full of doctors' appointments and second opinions. Every doctor said the same thing: Surgery or radiation was not an option because the cancer was already in Johnny's bones. The only thing they could offer us was continuous hormone therapy, which had mixed results, sometimes staving off the cancer for about two years.

Before we started hormone therapy treatment, we decided to try a holistic approach first. We went to Health Quarters in Colorado Springs for 11 days and did a complete body detox together. We came home, started juicing and eating a total vegan diet and did this for four months. I'm a firm believer in eating healthy foods, yet this course of action didn't reverse the drive of Johnny's cancer. In fact, the cancer was progressively getting worse. One of the indications of this came from a prostate-specific antigen (PSA) test. Larger amounts of PSA are released when the prostate gland is enlarged, infected or diseased. The higher the PSA, the more likely the presence or continuance of prostate cancer—anything over 10 is considered dangerous. Four months from Johnny's first diagnosis, his PSA had risen from an already whopping 48 to 65. Things did not look good.

We are forever grateful to the lady in First Place who sent me a video right after we received Johnny's diagnosis. On the video, a doctor in Los Angeles was speaking about prostate cancer. He didn't believe in continuous hormone therapy and gave his reasons why. We were intrigued with what Dr. Bob Leibowitz had to say, but we didn't see any way that we could go to California for medical care. I am so grateful that God had other plans. Dr. Bob said on the video that he used only 13 months of hormone therapy to treat his patients and then used other treatments. His survival statistics were extremely encouraging to us. We began hormone therapy treatment in Houston, and after 13 months decided to go to California and consult with Dr. Bob before doing anything further.

We were so taken by Dr. Bob's compassion and knowledge of the disease that we decided right then that he would become our primary caregiver. Dr. Bob is an oncologist who specializes in prostate cancer. Men go to him from all over the world. This was in the spring of 1999. Little did we know that God was going to provide First Place a publisher in Ventura, California, just an hour's drive from Los Angeles, in the fall of 2000!

133

Chronic, Yes; Despairing, No

We are thrilled and thankful that Johnny is alive and feeling well as I write these words, now eight years after his diagnosis.

But we are thankful for so much more than that. We're thankful that we no longer take a single day of our marriage for granted. I guess that we, like so many couples, thought that since we were both healthy, we would die of old age in our 90s! Without a disease like cancer coming into our lives, we don't believe that God would have been able to teach us so much about how precious each day is. We treasure every minute of every day we have together. We don't think twice about spending two hours on the pier together after dinner, even if we have things we need to do. We have even talked about the 45-mile drive I make to work each way. With the Houston traffic and Houston drivers, I could die before Johnny! Life is precious, and life is in the hands of our Lord.

Another thing we have learned, and that we are thankful for, is that we know that Johnny is not going to die until the Lord Jesus calls him home. We are as confident of this fact as we are about our next breath. Our lives are in God's hands, and that's the best possible place they could be.

134

Ever since our daughter Shari died in 2001, we are more excited about heaven than ever before because we will get to see her again. In fact, the older we get, the more family and friends we have on the other side. What a joyous reunion that will be when we all get to heaven!

Our cancer journey has been difficult and sometimes frustrating but never dull. No one could be more fun or more of a joy to be around than my precious Johnny. He never complains, never whines and is never angry about his cancer. He has never had a pity party or said, "Why me?" Cancer has only strengthened the love and bond we already had, and we are both blessed beyond measure to have whatever time either of us has left to be together.

Romans 8:35-39 sums it up for both Johnny and me:

Who shall separate us from the love of Christ? Shall trouble or hardship or persecution or famine or nakedness or danger or sword? As it is written: "For your sake we face death all day long; we are considered as sheep to be slaughtered." No, in all these things we are more than conquerors through him who loved us. For I am convinced that neither death nor life, neither angels nor demons, neither the present nor the future, nor any powers, neither height nor depth, nor anything else in all creation, will be able to separate us from the love of God that is in Christ Jesus our Lord.

Yes, our problem is ever-present. Cancer has not vanished from our lives. There are times, still, when Johnny is very sick. Yet God is an ever-present God, and His love carries us through.

Prayer

Dear Lord, how hard it is to give thanks when every day is filled with sickness. Yet You are Lord of all. Today we choose to give thanks, even in the midst of this situation. We cast upon You all anxiety, all frustration and fear. You are God, and You are good. Amen.

A Thankful Life

And we, who with unveiled faces all reflect the Lord's glory, are being transformed into his likeness with ever-increasing glory.

2 CORINTHIANS 3:18

On Thanksgiving night of 2001, our daughter Shari was struck by a drunk driver while standing in the driveway of her in-laws' home. She died a few hours later in a Houston hospital. Shari was 39 years old. Her death left Jeff, her husband of 20 years, without a wife, and their daughters, Amanda, 13, Christen, 15, and Cara, 19, without their mother.

On the third anniversary of my daughter's death, I drove into work with heavy fog and misting rain as my companions. The weather only added to my melancholy that I wasn't able to be with Jeff and the girls that day. I began praying for them and asking God to hold them close in His arms.

Undeniably, Shari's death has been the hardest thing our family has ever gone through. Though the days following her death were full of pain for all of us, I can also say with thankfulness that they are not a blur. Each day stands out with crystal clarity in my mind, even today. Because I keep a prayer journal, I have a record of everything that happened during that time. A week after Shari's death, I had written down 22 things for which to be thankful in the midst of this tragic time.

Here are some of the things I was thankful for during that time:

- Christian friends who were already at the hospital when we arrived and who never left our side.
- Jeff's mom and brother accepting Jesus Christ as Savior one hour after Shari's death.
- My granddaughter Cara witnessing about Jesus to the young girl who drove while drunk and whose car hit Shari.
- My friend Beth Moore being in town so that she was available to speak at Shari's service.
- Rick Jones, our minister of pastoral care, and his wife, Peggy, taking care of every detail of the viewing and burial, and thinking to film the service.
- My nephew, Rick Crawford, doing the music at Shari's service.
- Jeff's eloquent speaking at Shari's service.
- The poem my granddaughter Amanda wrote about her mom for Jeff to read.
- Jeff's sister, Yvonne, who spoke in front of an audience for the first time ever and doing it so eloquently at Shari's service.
- Shari's last words to Cara as they walked to the car: "Let's check the Internet when we get home and see if you've been accepted to A&M"

137

(Texas A&M University).

- Cara receiving her acceptance letter to Texas A & M the morning after her mom's death.
- God giving Cara three Christian roommates at A & M—one of whom was Katy, who had lost her Mom tragically just six months before.
- Sue Odom and Mary Vasquez, dear friends who drove from Yorktown, Texas, to cook and clean until the funeral was over.
- Deborah Collins, a friend and Mom's caretaker, who stayed around the clock to care for my mom until after the funeral.
- Finding in my closet a brand-new pantsuit that Lisa and Shari had given me the Christmas before. I wore it to the viewing. I had never worn it before because it was too tight when I received it. When I slipped it on, it fit perfectly.
- God's waking me that Thanksgiving morning and prodding me to get up so He could speak to me through the first chapter of James.
- Traveling with Shari to North Carolina just one month before her death.

At the time of Shari's death, I never dreamed that thankfulness might be one of the things God would use to heal the huge void left in my heart. I know that people grieve in different ways and that everyone is different, but I have come to believe that being thankful *in the midst of* a tragic circumstance is the key to moving toward healing.

Could thankfulness actually spare us from experiencing some of the stages of grief when we go through the hard times of our lives? I have been pondering this question during the last three years because I haven't experienced three of the five stages of grief over the death of my daughter. It is an accepted belief that most people experience five stages of grief: shock, denial, anger, bargaining and acceptance. I have waited for denial, anger and bargaining, thinking that I might be stuck in shock; but after three years, could thankfulness in the midst of a circumstance as shattering as the death of a child propel me from shock to acceptance without my having to experience the other three stages?

I shared what I believed God was teaching me about thankfulness with my friend Bev Henson and asked her if she thought this might have merit in light of God's Word. Bev said that in the Old Testament (see Lev. 13–14), lepers were required to go through many steps before being able to present themselves to the priest; but when the 10 lepers cried out to Jesus (see Luke 17:11-19), they were told to go and present themselves to the priest, bypassing the many steps. I find it quite interesting in this passage of Scripture that only 1 of the 10 lepers returned to thank Jesus. Ten were cleansed, but only one returned to give thanks.

Always Thankful, Always

Even though I accept my daughter's death, sadness still comes to me, like on the third anniversary of her death while driving in the dreary weather. As I drove into the church parking lot that morning, it was almost 6:00 A.M.—still dark. After I parked my car, I sat there for a moment, watching the rain.

I really miss Shari, I thought.

In my mind, the familiar words of 1 Thessalonians 5:18—the basis for this book—came to mind: "Give thanks in all circumstances, for this is God's will for you in Christ Jesus."

All circumstances.

All.

I know that the Lord is using something even as horrible as the death of Shari for His glory. It is something He allowed, though I'll never fully know why. In the process, He is using this experience to transform me, and many others, into the image of His Son. Because I know that God is perfect and God is good, I know that He uses all things for His ideal purposes. I can claim with confidence the words of 2 Corinthians 3:18—that "we, who with unveiled faces all reflect the Lord's glory, are being transformed into His likeness with ever-increasing glory."

While sitting in the parking lot, I began to give thanks.

I started thanking God for everything that came to mind. I thanked God that Jeff has sold the house that he and Shari were in the process of building when she died. I thanked God that the closing was that very day; and even though it would be bittersweet because of the date, it would also be sweet because God had been so faithful the past three years. I thanked God that Jeff's boss gave him six months leave of absence from work (with pay) to finish the house, and that his company has been patient for the house to sell so they could be repaid the money they advanced Jeff to finish it. I thanked God that Jeff would now have the money to pay for the wedding of his oldest daughter, Cara, in January 2005, because of the sale of the house. I thanked God that my husband, Johnny, is alive and doing well and that God has allowed him to live these past eight years with stage-four prostate cancer.

The rain stopped, and I got out of my car to go to the office.

An Available Antidote

Each and every one of us travels through seasons of difficulty in this life. The difficulty could be divorce; problems at home; problems with money; problems with parents, children or neighbors; problems with health. Though we have faith in the Lord of glory, that doesn't mean we'll be spared from all the harm and difficulty that can occur here on Earth.

Being thankful gives us the power to change our attitudes, no matter what we are going through. Thankfulness also affects our relationship with our Father God. As we thank Him for wherever we are right now, He comes through as our loving heavenly Father to soothe and heal our wounds.

Each of us has a choice to make when it comes to being thankful: We can stay trapped in our pain and anger over our losses or disappointments, or we can choose to thank God for whatever we can. The death of a loved one is probably the greatest loss any of us will ever face, but it is a sure fact that if we live long enough, we will all face a loss such as this.

My friend Martha Norsworthy, a First Place leader in Murray, Kentucky, suffered through the death of her only child, Carol, on December 22, 1993. Carol and her husband, Brian, were killed when a drunk driver struck the van they were driving. Carol and Brian had no children of their own, but they and their church had adopted the many poor and needy children in their community. The night of the accident, Carol and Brian were delivering Christmas gifts given by the members of their church to the families of these children.

During the days following Carol and Brian's death, I spent time talking with Martha by phone. I will never forget Martha relaying the things she was thankful for in their circumstance. She was thankful that their memory verse that week had been Hebrews 12:1: "Therefore, since we are surrounded by such a great cloud of witnesses, let us throw off everything that hinders and the sin that so easily entangles, and let us run with perseverance the race marked out for us." Martha said that she kept seeing the verse over and over again in her mind as though it were displayed on the billboard at her local bank. She realized that Carol and Brian were now in that great cloud of witnesses and they were both cheering her on to finish the race marked out for her. Martha was also thankful for Carol's and Brian's prayer journals from their First Place group. In the weeks following their deaths, she was comforted to see, as she read their journals, how much they had grown spiritually. She will be forever thankful that they both had been in her class during the fall session. Reading their prayers was her link with God and with them.

When we realize that God knows all about our suffering and that He loves us, we can cast our grief and pain on Him, because He cares for us.

143

A Thankful Life

Where are you today? Are you reeling from the death of a family member or a friend you loved? Maybe the death is a recent one, or it might have been 20 years ago; nevertheless, you are still reeling. Are you smarting over the sting of bankruptcy? Have your carefully laid plans changed in ways you never would have dreamed? Are you arguing with your teenager? Have you faced a diagnosis that will mean certain pain and discomfort, and possibly death?

I believe the hope and healing you so desperately need is found in the simple act of being thankful. Start thanking God for everything you can think of surrounding the death of your loved one and see how God begins to heal your heart. "Anger," "pain," "discouragement" and "despair" are antonyms to "thankfulness" and "praise."

As we begin practicing thankfulness today, God will begin an amazing transformation in our hearts. We can look forward to His promises, His plan and His glory.

Prayer

144

Dear Lord, help me see the things I can thank You for no matter what my circumstances are today. Flood my mind with Your presence and show me that You were there when these situations occurred and that You are here now. Wrap me in Your arms of love and start the healing of my fractured heart. Give me Your hope and the opportunities to share with others all the things You teach me in Your amazing plan for my life. Thank You. Amen.

Creating a Thankfulness Journal

O LORD my God, I will give you thanks forever.

PSALM 30:12

One of the easiest ways to foster an attitude of thankfulness is to create a thankfulness journal—a place to record the simple, everyday things for which you are grateful. Even though you may already record daily entries in a prayer journal or diary, keep a separate thankfulness journal to develop a heart that gives thanks in all circumstances.

Unlike other forms of journaling, a thankfulness journal has one purpose and one purpose only: to record the things for which you are thankful. It is both an acknowledgment of what God has done for you and a challenge to look for things to be thankful for, even on "bad" days. Practice recording daily the things God has done so that you won't miss the little things that can get lost in the busy-ness of life.

At first glance, keeping a written list of what you are thankful for may seem to be too simplistic to be effective. Yet study after study has proven the positive impact of maintaining a thankfulness journal. Researchers have discovered that those who keep thankfulness journals on a daily basis exercise more regularly, have fewer health problems and make greater progress toward important personal goals. Gratitude-journalers experience less depression and handle stress more effectively. In addition, they have more energy and vitality. They even sleep better at night! And spiritual masters throughout the ages have maintained that those with thankful hearts reap God's choicest blessings. In a society in which complexity seems to be preferred, it is amazing that something as simple as keeping a thankfulness journal can change one's quality of life so drastically! (Why not keep a thankfulness journal for at least two months and take stock of how your life has changed at the end of that time?)

Keeping a thankfulness journal is not only beneficial but it is also fun! Even on the "bad" days it becomes a mental challenge to sort through the events of life and find those simple pleasures we often overlook.

146

If creating a thankfulness journal sounds like something you would like to add to your spiritual disciplines, here are just a few basic steps that will put you on the road to hope and healing.

Keep It Simple

Unlike other spiritual journals, a thankfulness journal is not a place to process your feelings, cry out in lament or pour out your heart to God. The whole purpose of a thankfulness journal is to do one thing: give thanks. Thank God for blessing you in ways too numerous to ever adequately recount. This is the time to simply write, "I am thankful for _____" statements consisting of one or two sentences. Drawings, small photographs or mementos of special occasions that brought joy and gratitude into your life can be added to enrich your simple words.

Keep It Honest
There is absolutely no reason to exaggerate, minimize or force your feelings. List only the things for which you are genuinely grateful. God knows your thoughts before you even write them on the page (see Psalm 139:4). This is not a place for pious platitudes or lofty idealism. Heartfelt gratitude is always about the truth as it applies to your life in the present moment.

Keep It Personal

147

This thankfulness journal is about you and your relationship with God, not about your neighbor—so no comparing or judging others. Remember that the Pharisee Jesus criticized prayed, "God, I thank you that I am not like other men" (Luke 18:11). We never need to fill our cup of thankfulness to overflowing by devaluing another human being in an attempt to feed our ego. God is never pleased with such a phony show of gratitude. Gratitude is not about what we have done for God; it's about giving thanks to Him for the wonderful things He has done for us.

Keep It Specific
Rather than writing generalized statements such as "I am thankful that God is faithful," record a specific instance that reminded you of God's faithfulness.

Perhaps you saw or heard something today that brought God's lovingkindness to memory. Write down the thing that made you remember instead of stating that you are thankful for God's lovingkindness. Instead of being thankful for the sun, write about how the sun touched your skin and brought warmth to your soul.

Keep It Consistent

Make adding entries to your thankfulness journal a daily habit. Begin by writing down five simple pleasures for which you are thankful each morning when you first wake up. At the end of the day, before you go to bed, record another five things that happened that day for which you are thankful. Five entries in the morning, five in the evening, seven days a week; such a small investment will accumulate 70 entries each week! Try not to repeat the same list day after day. Each day is a unique gift from God, and each day is filled with its own special blessings.

Perhaps you're thinking, *I couldn't possibly find 70 things to be thankful for each week.* But remember that you are training your mind in order to develop a lifestyle of thankfulness. The scarcity mentality that tells us we will not have enough and the fear of not having enough thankfulness to write 70 "I am thankful" sentences each month hit at the very heart of the problem. Just focus on writing down five in the morning and five in the evening—today—and trust that there will be five in the morning and five in the evening again tomorrow. Write the date on each page and keep them in date order.

Start It Now

Any kind of notebook will suffice for a thankfulness journal. The important thing is that your gratitude pages are bound together and kept in a safe place rather than randomly scribbled on loose pieces of paper scattered here and there. Some folks like to decorate the cover of their thankfulness journal; others like to draw pictures that describe the things and events for which they are thankful. Stationery stores, arts and crafts retailers, and vendors of scrapbooking supplies allow you to customize your journal and add to the creativity and individuality of the project. The more unique and creative the pages, the more likely you may be to visit the journal daily and stay committed to consistent entries. (Of course, you may be a minimalist about decorated covers and want to simply keep a journal filled with writing—no art needed.) Most people find they want enough room in the journal to keep two or thee month's worth of gratitude affirmations.

149

One More Tip

A Scripture heading placed at the top of each day's page will remind you of the One to whom you are thankful. Searching the Scriptures for thankfulness verses can also become part of your lifestyle-of-thankfulness journey. Committing some of these thankfulness verses to memory is an important part of the transformation that will take place as you express your thankfulness to God through the pages of your thankfulness journal.

Be sure to reread your thankfulness entries often, especially on days when you need to be reminded of God's faithful love. On a day when life is dark and gloomy, you can begin your thankfulness entries by thanking God that He has given you the grace to keep a thankfulness journal to read!

God delights in those who delight in Him, and He showers them with His abundant blessings.

Note

1. Robert A. Emmons and Michael E. McCullough, "Highlights from the Research Project on Gratitude and Thankfulness—Dimensions and Perspectives of Gratitude." http://www.psy.miami.edu/faculty/mmccullough/Gratitude-Related%20 Stuff/highlights_fall_2003.pdf (accessed July 2005).

WORKSHEET 1

Help to Get Started

Use the following questions to help you begin thinking about thankfulness in the manner described. Once you have created your unique thankfulness journal, transfer the entries you have made in this worksheet to the first page of your journal.

- Write a short statement expressing your thankfulness to God for a simple pleasure.
- Draw a small picture next to your sentence that creatively expresses your gratitude.
- What private thanksgiving would you like to share with God? Share it now!
- Write a thankfulness truth that applies to your life in the present moment.
- List one great thing that God has done for you that fills you with joy.
- What recent occurrence in your life reminds you of God's lovingkindness? Write it down as a thank offering.
- Think of something you have done today that you can't write about with thankfulness. Now thank God that He forgives you for doing that specific thing.

Using a topical concordance, make a list of the seven

Scripture verses you will use as the daily headings in your thankfulness journal this week. If you don't have a topical concordance, you can find many Bible verses that express thankfulness in the prayers at the end of each day's Bible study lesson throughout this book.

1.

2.

3.

4.

5.

6.

7.

Which one of these verses will you commit to memory this week?

Journal Sample Page

Don't Miss the
Bible Study Companion
to *A Thankful Heart*

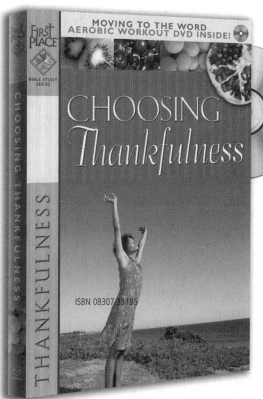

Includes *Moving to the Word Aerobic Workout* DVD!

Choosing Thankfulness
First Place
Bible Study

For those struggling with out-of-control eating habits, meditating on God's attributes, His promises and His unfailing love gives rise to joy and thanksgiving. Explore the Scriptures and be encouraged by the examples of men and women who were able to thank God in adversity and sorrow because they remembered Jehovah's promise to be their Lord.

Also from Carole Lewis

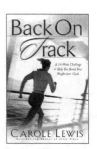

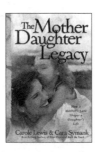
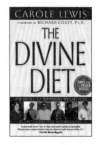

BIBLE STUDIES FOR
A HEALTHY LIFESTYLE

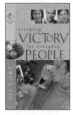